Step–by–Step
Kids' Birthday
Cakes

Step-by-Step
Kids' Birthday
Cakes

Karen Sullivan

LONDON, NEW YORK, MELBOURNE,
MUNICH, AND DELHI

Project Editor Kathy Woolley
Designer Harriet Yeomans
Managing Editor Dawn Henderson
Managing Art Editor Christine Keilty
Jacket Art Editor Kathryn Wilding
Senior Producer, Pre-Production Tony Phipps
Senior Producer Jen Scothern
Art Director Peter Luff
Publisher Peggy Vance
US Consultant Kate Curnes Ramos
US Editor Jenny Siklos
US Senior Editor Margaret Parrish

Cake Decorators Sandra Monger, Hannah
Wiltshire, Kasey Clarke, Juniper Cakery

DK INDIA
Project Editor Bushra Ahmed
Senior Art Editor Ira Sharma
Editor Ligi John
Art Editor Simran Kaur
Assistant Art Editor Sourabh Challariya
Managing Editor Alicia Ingty
Managing Art Editor Navidita Thapa
Pre-Production Manager Sunil Sharma
DTP Designers Rajdeep Singh,
Manish Upreti, Mohammad Usman

First American Edition, 2014
Published in the United States by DK Publishing
4th floor, 345 Hudson Street
New York, New York 10014

14 15 16 17 18 10 9 8 7 6 5 4 3 2 1
001—259429—September/2014

Copyright © 2014 Dorling Kindersley Limited

ISBN: 978-1-4654-2102-9

DK books are available at special discounts when purchased in
bult for sales promotions, premiums, fund-raising, or
educational use. For details, contact:
DK Publishing Special Markets, 345 Hudson Street,
New York, New York 10014 or SpecialSales@dk.com.

Color reproduction by Altaimage LTD
Printed and bound in South China

Discover more at **www.dk.com**

Contents

Introduction

It's never been easier to bake and decorate delicious, imaginative, and truly child-friendly cakes, and with all the ingredients and tools you need now readily available, even amateur decorators can create show-stopping cakes, cupcakes, and cake pops with ease. There is something hugely satisfying about producing homemade creations, designed to match a party theme and your child's individual interests, and this book offers not just detailed, step-by-step instructions to achieve something truly spectacular, but inspiration for producing your own designs and variations, too.

Everything from **basic baking techniques**, leveling, frosting, and filling cakes to delicious recipes, covering a cake drum, dipping and decorating cake pops and producing perfect cupcakes is given the step-by-step treatment. Twenty amazing **cake projects**, complete with variations and suggestions for goody bags or additional treats to enhance your theme, top the bill, and you'll discover how to create an astonishing range of children's birthday cakes from scratch.

Everyone from absolute beginners to seasoned experts will find cakes to suit their level of skill and experience, and inspiration to produce their own creations. If you want to make something easy but stunning, you'll love the gorgeous Sparkly Butterfly, Fish Tank Friends, Up, Up, and Away, Cupcake Owl, Cupcake Caterpillar, Over the Rainbow, Soccer Mania, Treasure Island, Over the Moon, and Monster Madness cakes. Bakers with a little more time on their hands will find the stunning In the Jungle, Pretty Fairies, Dinosaur Egg, Flying Superhero, Circus Big Top, Party Train, Princess Castle, Happy Robot, Prima Ballerina, and Furry Teddy Bear cakes a satisfying challenge. You'll find cakes for soccer fans, monster-crazed tots, budding superheroes, train buffs, space fanatics, dinosaur hunters, shipwrecked pirates, robot engineers, and even fairy princesses. Choose your cake, gather your equipment and ingredients, and we'll guide you through every step until you achieve the cake of your child's dreams.

You'll find inspiring ideas for cake pops, cupcakes, and round cakes on the dedicated **feature pages**, as well as a number of 10-minute transformations that will help you produce a masterpiece with a few simple ideas (and shortcuts). Now is the time to learn how to bake and decorate cakes that will please a crowd and thrill the birthday boy or girl.

Enjoy!

Cake Chooser

From simple projects to... > > > > > > > > > > > >

Cupcake Caterpillar *p142*

Sparkly Butterfly *p126*

Cupcake Owl *p82*

Up, Up, and Away *p21*

Monster Madness *p12*

Fish Tank Friends *p116*

Over the Rainbow *p60*

Soccer Mania *p96*

Prima Ballerina *p104*

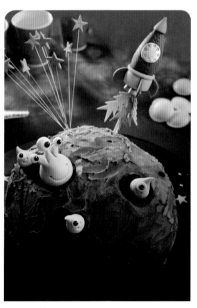

Over the Moon *p34*

Happy Robot *p120*

Flying Superhero *p154*

Dinosaur Egg *p74*

Treasure Island *p50*

Furry Teddy Bear *p42*

>>>>>>>>> >... more adventurous creations

Princess Castle *p146*

Party Train *p66*

Pretty Fairies *p20*

Circus Big Top *p130*

In the Jungle *p86*

Monster Madness

Frighten your party guests with this cute six-eyed monster, complete with piped buttercream fur, a bright green nose, fierce teeth, and neat little toes. The cake is stacked, but does not need dowels for support. Accompany with the monster cupcakes on page 18—if you dare.

 PREP 1½ hrs   **BAKE** 2 hrs   **DECORATE** 2¼ hrs, plus overnight drying time   **SERVES** 30

Ingredients

- 4 x 8in (20cm) round vanilla sponge cakes (see p164)
- 7in (18cm) vanilla sponge cake
- 2lb 3oz (1kg) vanilla buttercream frosting
- cornstarch, for dusting
- 10oz (300g) bright blue fondant, strengthened
- orange food coloring paste
- 9oz (250g) white candy melts
- 6 x 1oz (30g) cake pops
- 3½oz (100g) orange candy melts
- 1¾oz (50g) black fondant
- 1¾oz (50g) white fondant
- 3½oz (100g) green fondant, strengthened

Equipment

- 12in (30cm) cake board
- palette knife
- 12in (30cm) round cake drum
- fondant roller and smoother
- sharp knife
- large star piping tip (such as Wilton no. 48)
- large piping bag
- 9 cake-pop sticks
- styrofoam block (optional)
- 1¼in (3cm) circular cutter
- 3¼ft (1m) green satin ribbon, ½in (1cm) wide
- craft glue

1 To construct the layers, place one of the 8in (20cm) sponge cakes on the cake board. Using a palette knife, cover the top with a layer of frosting, then place the second cake on it. Continue until you have stacked all four 8in (20cm) cakes. Apply a layer of frosting to the top of the stack and position the smaller cake on it. Crumb coat the entire cake with frosting (see pp170–1) and set aside overnight.

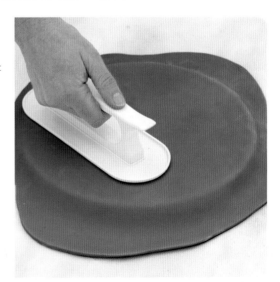

2 To cover the cake drum, dust a surface with cornstarch and roll out the bright blue fondant in a circle large enough to cover the cake drum— it should be about ⅛in (3mm) thick. Brush the drum with water and then carefully smooth the fondant over the surface (see pp178–9). Polish with the fondant smoother and cut off any excess using a sharp knife. Allow to dry overnight.

3 Move the cake to the covered drum. Color the remaining buttercream frosting using the orange food coloring paste (see p180). Attach a star tip to the end of the piping bag and fill with the orange buttercream. Starting at the base, pipe the "fur" by pressing the bag, releasing the pressure, and pulling the frosting outward to get a nice point. Pipe moving upward to the top edge until the cake is covered. Continue piping over the top, paying particular attention to the edges, which should appear rounded. Set aside.

4 For the eyeballs, melt the white candy melts. Put the cake-pop sticks into the cake pops (see p173) and dip into the candy, coating evenly. Stand them up in a piece of styrofoam, or an overturned colander, until they harden.

5 Melt the orange candy melts and dip the cake pops into the liquid so that they are half covered, to form the appearance of eyelids. Stand them upright again, until they are dry and hard.

Use water to affix each circle under the lid.

6 Dust a surface with cornstarch and roll out the black fondant to ⅛in (3mm) thick. Cut out six circles with the circular cutter and affix one on each cake pop under the lid.

7 Re-roll the remaining black fondant to about ⅛in (3mm) thick. Use a sharp knife to cut out and shape a mouth, about 4in (10cm) long and 1½in (4cm) wide. Set aside.

Arrange the teeth in a random manner to give the monster a scary appearance.

8 Dust the surface again with cornstarch and roll out a bit of the white fondant to about ⅛in (3mm) thick. Using a sharp kdnife, cut 3–5 triangles for the teeth. Brush the backs of the teeth with a little water and attach onto the mouth.

9 To make the toes, roll four cherry-sized balls and two slightly larger balls from the strengthened green fondant. Strengthen the remaining white fondant (see p176), and roll it into six pea-sized balls. Shape these balls into curved, pointed claws. Brush the wider ends with a little water and affix to the toes. Let dry, ideally overnight.

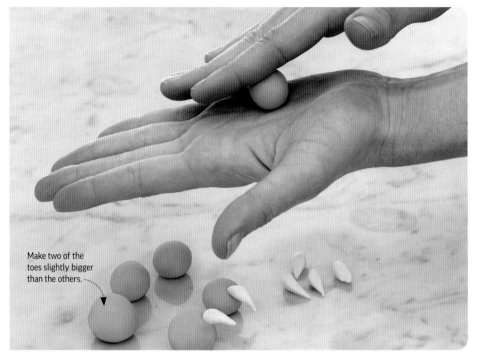

Make two of the toes slightly bigger than the others.

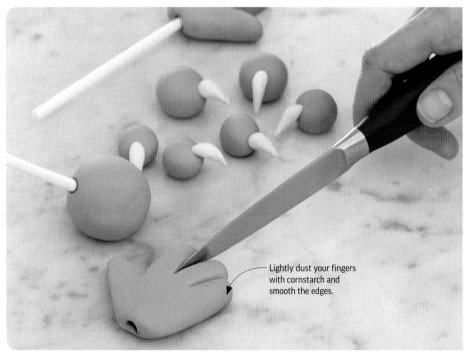

Lightly dust your fingers with cornstarch and smooth the edges.

10 To make the nose, roll a golf-ball-sized sphere of the green fondant and insert a cake-pop stick halfway into the ball. Set aside. For the hands, roll the remaining green fondant into two walnut-sized balls and flatten slightly with the fondant roller. Cut out the fingers using a sharp knife. Moisten one end of two cake-pop sticks with a little water and insert into the wrist of each hand. Set aside to harden, ideally overnight.

Insert the eyes at uneven angles.

Insert the hands on the sides, making sure the cake-pop sticks are not visible.

11 Moisten the back of the mouth with water and gently position on the cake. To fix the nose, moisten the stick attatched to the nose and insert into the cake. Insert the cake-pop eyes into the top of the cake. Attach the green ribbon around the base of the cake drum, using a little craft glue.

Position the toes in a neat row at the base of the cake, as shown.

Monster Face Cupcakes

Using the star tip, pipe brightly colored buttercream frosting on to the cupcakes (see pp174–5), using the same technique as on the cake, to create furry buttercream monster faces. Use scraps of white fondant and strengthened colored fondant to create scary teeth, eyes,

noses, tentacles, and anything else that will capture your own little monsters' attention. Allow the fondant to set a little before applying to the cupcakes with water or edible glue. To provide contrast, use a palette knife to smooth the buttercream frosting onto some cupcakes.

Create tentacles or horns using bright-colored fondants.

Use the tip of a piping tip to score the horns.

Sandwich disks of white and black fondant onto cake-pop sticks for ghoulish eye stalks.

Triangles cut from white fondant can be used to create sharp fangs

Experiment with different piping tips to create crazy fur effects with brightly colored buttercream.

Strengthened fondant balls or candy-coated sweets can be used to create noses.

Pretty Fairies

This delicate cake is frosted with soft green buttercream frosting and topped with two adorable fairies, seated on fondant toadstools. Rice-paper butterflies, toadstools, and pastel blossoms are dotted around the cake and the drum, and a pretty hand-painted pattern runs around the base.

PREP 1 hr   **BAKE** 35 mins   **DECORATE** 4–4½ hrs, plus overnight drying time   **SERVES** 20

Ingredients

- 2½ cups (28oz/800g) buttercream, tinted pale green (see p180)
- 2 x 8in (20cm) round vanilla sponge cakes (see p164), sandwiched with buttercream and crumb coated (see p171)
- dry spaghetti
- edible black pen
- cornstarch, for dusting
- edible luster dust: pink, dark green, medium green, sage green, and lilac
- grain alcohol
- 4 sheets edible rice paper
- edible glitter
- ½ cup royal icing (see p181)
- yellow food coloring paste
- 1oz (25g) dark green fondant, strengthened (see p176)

For the fairies

- 3½oz (100g) flesh-colored fondant, strengthened
- 3½oz (100g) lilac fondant, strengthened
- 3½oz (100g) yellow fondant, strengthened
- 3½oz (100g) white fondant, strengthened
- 1¾oz (50g) pale-green fondant, strengthened

continued on the next page...

1 Paddle about a quarter of the pale-green buttercream frosting onto the cake drum and smooth using a palette knife. To get an even surface, dip the knife into warm water, dry, and smooth over the frosting. Set the drum aside for the frosting to firm.

2 Set the crumb-coated cake on a sheet of parchment paper. Using the palette knife, apply the remaining pale-green buttercream, and then use the side scraper to achieve a smooth surface. Put to one side, ideally overnight.

- 1oz (25g) brown
  fondant, strengthened
- 1oz (25g) orange
  fondant, strengthened

For the toadstools
- 5½oz (150g) red
  fondant, strengthened
- 5½oz (150g) bright pink
  fondant, strengthened

Equipment
- 10in (25cm) cake drum
- palette knife
- side scraper
- sharp knife
- styrofoam
- drinking straw cut vertically
  in half, or smile tool
- fondant roller
- blossom plunger cutters:
  extra large, large, medium,
  and small (see p187 for templates)
- toothpick
- small star plunger cutter
- small fine scissors
- small artist's paintbrush
- wheel tool
- 2 piping bags
- round small and medium piping
  tips (Wilton no. 1 and 4)
- ball tool
- small daisy plunger cutter
- 3¼ft (1m) green satin ribbon,
  ½in (1cm) wide
- craft glue

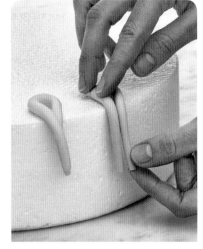

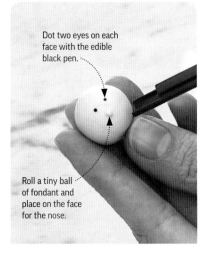

Dot two eyes on each
face with the edible
black pen.

Roll a tiny ball
of fondant and
place on the face
for the nose.

3 For the fairies, roll two long, thin
sausages of the flesh-colored fondant
and fold each into a U-shape to create
two sets of legs. Cut the ends flat, and
then place on a piece of styrofoam,
carefully arranging the legs so that they
are crossed.

4 Roll two cherry-sized balls of the
flesh-colored fondant for the heads.
Score a smile using the drinking straw.
For the bodies, model two bigger
oval-shaped balls of the fondant. Insert a
short length of spaghetti into each,
leaving a bit protruding from the neck.

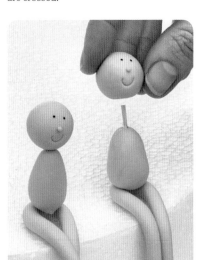

5 Affix the body of each fairy on one
set of legs. Poke a hole in the base of
each of the heads by placing them on the
spaghetti tips protruding from the top of
the body. Remove the heads and let
dry overnight.

6 For the dresses, dust a surface with
cornstarch and roll out some of the
lilac and yellow fondant to ¹⁄₁₆in (2mm)
thick. Using the extra-large blossom
cutter, cut out the skirts and score their
edges using the toothpick.

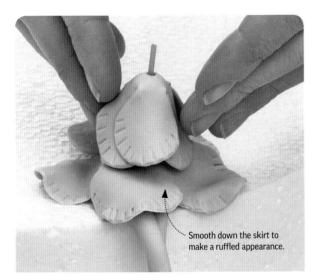

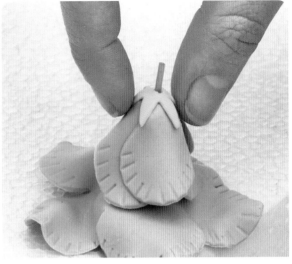

Smooth down the skirt to make a ruffled appearance.

7 Cut a hole in the center of the lilac skirt and slip it over the body. Dress the second fairy with the yellow skirt. Cut out the bodice from the lilac fondant using the large blossom cutter, and score the edges with a toothpick. Slip this over the body of the lilac fairy. Make a bodice for the yellow fairy using white fondant in the same way.

8 Dust a surface with cornstarch and roll out the pale green fondant very thinly. Using the star plunger cutter, cut out two star collars and slip one over the top of the bodice of each fairy.

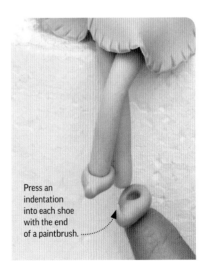

Press an indentation into each shoe with the end of a paintbrush.

9 Roll two more long, narrow sausages of flesh-colored fondant and cut each in half for the arms. Carefully flatten one end of each of the arms to create hands, and snip a thumb in each hand using the scissors.

10 Slip the head onto the protruding end of spaghetti. Moisten the tops of the arms with a little water and attach to the body, curving the arms and hands into position.

11 Roll two pea-sized balls of the lilac fondant and form into tiny pointed shoes. Moisten the bottom of the legs with a little water and fit into the shoes. Create yellow fondant shoes for the yellow fairy.

Pretty Fairies 23

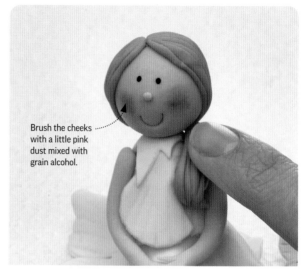

Brush the cheeks with a little pink dust mixed with grain alcohol.

12 For the hair, model narrow, tapered ropes of brown fondant and affix to the lilac fairy's head with a little water, with the wider ends at the crown, making a side part. Use the wheel tool to score the surface and create individual strands, and twist and curl the hair at the base.

13 For the yellow fairy, cut two small circles of orange fondant and attach to the head with a little water. Score the surface with the wheel tool. Model a ponytail, score the surface, and affix to the back of the head at the base of the hair with a little water, and position so that it falls over one shoulder.

14 For the wings, cut out two butterfly shapes from the rice paper and dust around the edges with edible glitter. Fold in half and then open each set of wings. Pipe a line of royal icing at the fold and affix to the back of the fairies.

15 Cut out 6–7 smaller butterfly shapes from the remaining rice paper. Dust with edible glitter, fold in half, then open the wings so that they are gently curved upward.

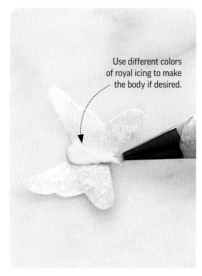

Use different colors of royal icing to make the body if desired.

Press the ball tool into the underside of each dome to create a cavity.

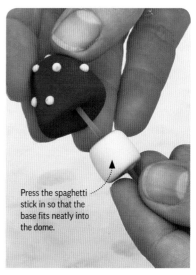

Press the spaghetti stick in so that the base fits neatly into the dome.

16 Tint a little of the royal icing yellow (see p181). Fit a piping bag with the no. 4 tip, fill with the yellow icing, and pipe the icing on the butterflies for the body. Let harden.

17 For the toadstools, use some of the red fondant to create 6–7 cherry-sized domes to dot around the cake. Repeat using some of the bright pink fondant to make 6–7 more domes.

18 Pipe tiny dots of royal icing on the domes, and dry for 30 minutes. Form the bases using white fondant, press a piece of spaghetti into them, and affix the domes on top.

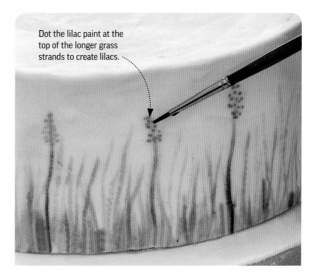

Dot the lilac paint at the top of the longer grass strands to create lilacs.

19 Use the remaining red fondant to create a larger dome for the lilac fairy to sit on. Pipe tiny dots on it using royal icing. Let dry and insert a piece of spaghetti into it, so it protrudes from both ends. Make a large dome using the bright pink fondant for the yellow fairy, dot with royal icing, and insert the spaghetti. Let dry, ideally overnight.

20 Carefully center the cake on the drum. Mix together the dark green luster dust with grain alcohol and stipple foliage around the base of the cake. Repeat with the medium- and sage-green luster dusts, until the base is covered. Mix the lilac luster dust with grain alcohol and create sprigs of tiny flowers on the cake using the paintbrush.

Pretty Fairies 25

21 To create flowers, dust a surface with cornstarch and roll out the remaining pink fondant very thinly. Using the medium and small blossom plunger cutters, cut out several little flowers. Gently curve the petals with the ball tool and pipe a dot of royal icing in the center. Repeat with the yellow and lilac fondant until you have cut about 50 flowers.

22 On the same surface, roll out the remaining white fondant very thinly. Using the daisy plunger cutter, cut out about 60 daisies. Gently curve the petals with the ball tool and pipe a dot of the yellow royal icing in the centers.

23 Using the dark green fondant, roll about 60 teardrop-shaped leaves. Point their tips using your fingers, and score with a knife to create veins.

24 To assemble the cake, press the large toadstools into the top so that the bottom length of spaghetti goes into the cake. Dot a little royal icing on the top of the toadstools, around the spaghetti protruding from the surface, and sit the fairies on top.

25 Dot the base of the other toadstools with water and arrange on the cake and the cake drum. Affix the flowers and leaves in pretty patterns on the cake and the cake drum using a little water.

Pretty Fairies

26 Use royal icing to attach the butterflies to the cake in a random pattern. Affix a yellow flower on the hair of the yellow fairy and a lilac flower on the lilac fairy with water.

Fairytale Cupcakes

Create beautiful fairy cupcakes (see pp174–175) to accompany your magical display. Simply pipe yellow buttercream onto the surface of the cupcakes, using a large, open-star nozzle, and set to one side. Model a series of miniature toadstools, as shown in steps 17–18, and let dry before pressing into the buttercream. Cut out tiny blossoms in a variety of pastel colors using the small blossom plunger cutters, and pipe white royal icing in the center.

Cut out rice paper butterflies, sprinkle with edible glitter, and fit with piped royal icing bodies before carefully displaying on the buttercream frosting. Any combination of cake decorations will produce exquisite cupcakes, so use your imagination and a liberal dusting of "fairy dust" glitter.

27 Wrap the green satin ribbon around the cake drum and affix in place using the craft glue.

Press the fondant toadstools onto the buttercream to decorate.

Up, Up, and Away

Multicolored fondant-covered cupcakes form a gorgeous balloon cake, with a modeled teddy bear in a basket below. An easy cake with high impact, it uses straws to link the balloon cupcakes to the blue-sky cupcakes. You can include as many, or as few, cupcakes as you wish.

 PREP 1 hr    **BAKE** 15 mins    **DECORATE** 1-1½ hrs, plus overnight drying time   **SERVES** 24

Ingredients

- confectioner's sugar, for dusting
- 3½oz (100g) medium-brown fondant, strengthened (see p176)
- 3½oz (100g) light-brown fondant, strengthened
- 1oz (25g) dark-brown fondant
- 3½oz (100g) each yellow, orange, green, purple, and bright-blue fondant
- 2½oz (75g) red fondant
- 2½oz (75g) fuchsia fondant
- 5½oz (150g) pale-blue fondant
- ⅔ cup (7oz/200g) buttercream frosting (see p180)
- 24 vanilla cupcakes (see pp164)
- ¼ cup royal icing (see p181)

Equipment

- fondant roller and smoother
- sharp knife
- blade tool
- small artist's paintbrush
- small round piping tip (such as Wilton no. 8)
- Dresden tool
- toothpick
- 3in (7.5cm) circular cutter
- palette knife
- piping bag
- 6 straws

1 To make the basket, dust a surface with confectioner's sugar and roll out the medium-brown fondant to ⅛in (3mm) thick. Using the sharp knife, cut a basket shape—5in (12cm) at the top, 4in (10cm) at the bottom, and 3½in (9cm) high. Wrap the remaining fondant in plastic wrap for later use.

2 Using the blade tool, score horizontal lines across the surface, leaving about ½in (1cm) unscored at the top of the basket. Score a series of diagonal slashes on the top of the basket and set aside to harden.

Attach the ears and muzzle to the head with a little water.

Roll three tiny balls of dark-brown fondant for the eyes and nose.

Use the end of a paintbrush to create a cavity in the ears.

Moisten the nose with a little water and attach to the face above the muzzle.

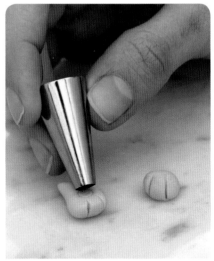

3 For the teddy bear, mold a walnut-sized ball of light-brown fondant for the head, and two tiny balls for the ears. Flatten the ears with your fingers, and create a cavity. Roll out a ball for the muzzle and flatten slightly. Attach the ears and muzzle to the head. Create eye sockets using the end of a paintbrush. Make the eyes and nose out of the dark-brown fondant, and place on the face. Set aside while you make the hands.

4 Form a small sausage of the light-brown fondant for the waving arm, shaping a round paw. Shape a second paw to peep over the basket. Using the blade tool, score lines on the paws, and use the piping tip to score a circle on the waving paw.

Use the Dresden tool to score a smile on the muzzle.

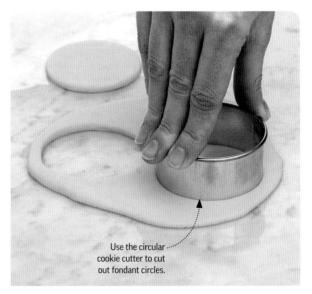

Use the circular cookie cutter to cut out fondant circles.

5 Use the toothpick to create stitch marks that run from the nose to the back of the head, between the ears. Attach the head and paws of the teddy bear to the basket using a little water, as shown on page 28. Let dry overnight.

6 Dust a surface with confectioner's sugar, roll out the yellow fondant to $1/8$in (4mm) thick, and cut three circles. Repeat to cut three orange, three green, three purple, three bright-blue, two red, two fuchsia, and five pale-blue circles.

7 Use the palette knife to smooth a thin layer of buttercream frosting on the cupcakes, about $\frac{1}{16}$in (2mm) thick and not quite covering the surface. Moisten the backs of the fondant circles with a little water and press onto the surface of the frosted cupcakes. Use the fondant smoother to create a smooth top.

Mini Balloon Cupcakes

Create miniature balloons to sit on top of cloud cupcakes for an extra treat. Simply dip cake pops into white candy melts (see p173), or melted white chocolate, and then quickly roll in a bowl of sprinkles. Press three or four toothpicks (taking care to snip off the sharp ends) into each of the candy-covered pops, and let set.

Once hard, invert and press into the cloud cupcakes (see step 8). You can also create balloons from cake pops dipped in a variety of brightly colored candy melts to liven up your display. Or make some tiny fondant teddy bears or baskets to sit under the balloon.

8 To make the sky, use the small piping tip to pipe little dots of royal icing close together on the blue cupcakes to form cloud shapes. Pipe a border around them using the same tip. Let set before serving. Arrange the cupcakes on a board or a cake plate, as shown on page 28.

10-minute *transformations*

You can transform a basic cake in just minutes with these simple but effective ideas. Start with a sponge cake frosted with buttercream then create the perfect party centerpiece with a selection of store-bought candies and toys, a little imagination, and a lot of style.

Toy teddy bears

Licorice candy sandwiches

square of ready-made fondant with colored rice-papered polka dots

store-bought wafer flowers and leaves

Teddy bears' picnic

Multicolored sprinkles

star picks

Use a large, round piping tip

Arrange store-bought stars on the buttercream while it's wet

Starry sky

Arrange the candies into colors before you start to decorate

Press in rows or in a random pattern if you're really short on time

sprinkles

Eat a rainbow

store-bought tinsel picks

Chocolate buttercream piped through a star tip

sprinkles

Sparkler surprise

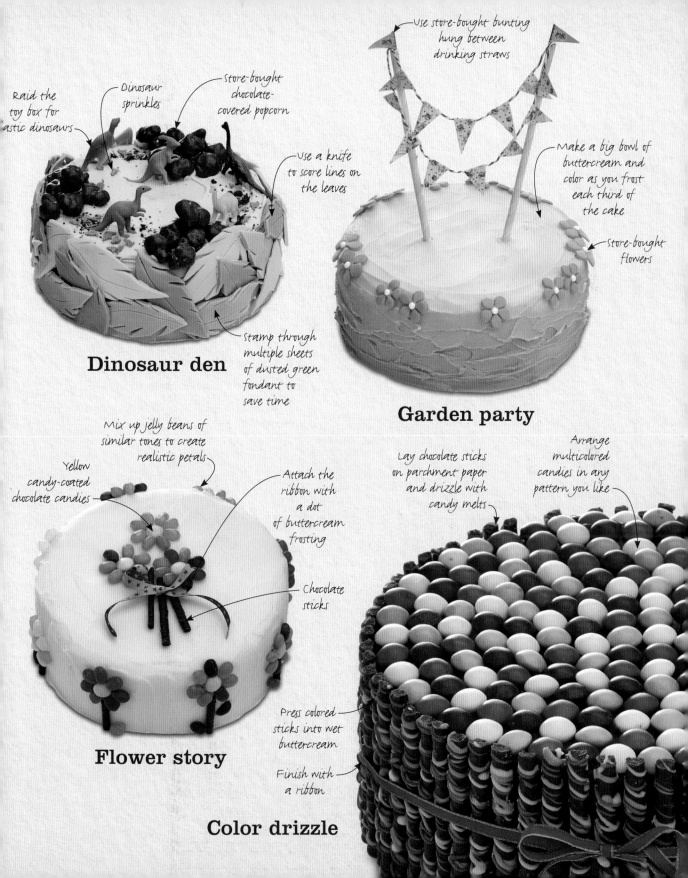

Dinosaur den

Raid the toy box for astic dinosaurs

Dinosaur sprinkles

Store-bought chocolate-covered popcorn

Use a knife to score lines on the leaves

stamp through multiple sheets of dusted green fondant to save time

Garden party

Use store-bought bunting hung between drinking straws

Make a big bowl of buttercream and color as you frost each third of the cake

Store-bought flowers

Flower story

Mix up jelly beans of similar tones to create realistic petals

Yellow candy-coated chocolate candies

Attach the ribbon with a dot of buttercream frosting

Chocolate sticks

Color drizzle

Lay chocolate sticks on parchment paper and drizzle with candy melts

Arrange multicolored candies in any pattern you like

Press colored sticks into wet buttercream

Finish with a ribbon

Over the Moon

Blast off with this fabulous space cake, accessorized with planetary cake pops, eerie green aliens, and glittery gold stars. The fondant rocket is easy to make and will last for months in an airtight container, so your little space travelers can admire it long after the festivities have ended.

 PREP 1 hr    **BAKE** 45 mins    **DECORATE** 3¾ hrs, plus overnight drying time   **SERVES** 20

Ingredients

- cornstarch, for dusting
- 1lb 2oz (500g) black fondant
- 7oz (200g) yellow fondant
- gold luster dust mixed with grain alcohol, or gold luster spray (optional)
- silver dragées
- 4 cups (2lb 3oz/1kg) vanilla buttercream, half tinted dark gray, half tinted light gray
- 8in (20cm) dome cake (see p187) (made in half of a hemisphere or ball pan), crumb coated with buttercream (see pp170–1)

For the aliens
- 1lb 2oz (500g) alien green fondant, strengthened
- dry spaghetti
- 1oz (25g) white fondant
- 1oz (25g) black fondant

For the rocket
- 1 oz (25g) red fondant, strengthened
- 3½oz (100g) blue fondant, strengthened
- 1oz (25g) gray fondant, strengthened
- 1oz (25g) yellow fondant, strengthened
- silver luster spray

continued on the next page...

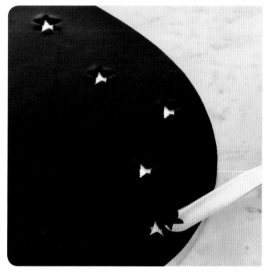

1 Using a fondant roller, roll the black fondant to about ⅛in (3mm) thick in a circle large enough to cover the drum. Brush the drum lightly with water and cover with the fondant (see p179). Cut off any excess with a sharp knife and reserve the remaining fondant. Carefully cut out about 15 stars from around the edge of the circle, using the star cutter. Lift them from the drum using a palette knife and discard.

2 To make the aliens, mold a cherry-sized ball of the strengthened alien green fondant into a cone and then model into a gentle teardrop shape. Repeat to make three aliens. To create the larger alien, use a golf-ball-sized ball of green fondant and mold into a teardrop shape. Using scissors, snip three peaks on the top and use your fingers to smooth.

- 2 tbsp (25g) royal icing
- 1oz (25g) orange fondant

Equipment

- fondant roller and smoother
- 12in (30cm) cake drum
- sharp knife
- ⅜in (1.2cm) star cutter
- palette knife
- 4 circular cutters—¾in (1.2cm), 1½in (4cm), 1in (2.5cm), and ¼in (5mm)
- small round piping tip (such as Wilton no. 2)
- small artist's paintbrush
- cake-pop stick
- 10 x 24-gauge silver wires
- 3¼ft (1m) black satin ribbon, ½in (1cm) wide
- craft glue
- plastic flower pick

3 Insert small pieces of dry spaghetti into the peaks to create spikes. These will support the eyeballs. Use a circular cutter to emboss smiles on the aliens. The end of a paintbrush can be used to mark the corners of the aliens' mouths.

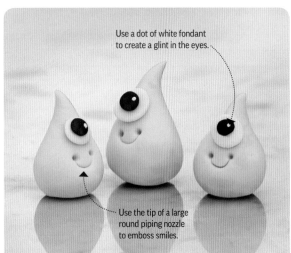

Use a dot of white fondant to create a glint in the eyes.

Use the tip of a large round piping nozzle to emboss smiles.

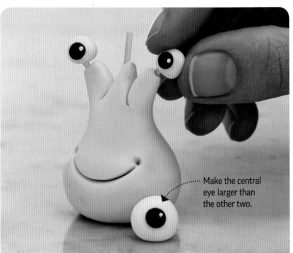

Make the central eye larger than the other two.

4 Roll three small balls of white fondant, flatten slightly, and attach to the aliens, using a little water, to create eyes. Press a smaller flattened ball of black fondant onto the surface of each ball of white fondant. Add a tiny dot of white fondant over the black fondant to create a glint in their eyes. Let dry overnight.

5 For the larger alien, roll three balls of strengthened white fondant to create eyeballs, and use the same technique as in step 4 to complete the eyes. Let dry overnight, or until slightly hardened. When the eyeballs are firm, press them down on the alien spikes, holding them in place until they feel secure. Allow to set.

Use the end of a piping tip to mark holes down either side of the lines.

6 Begin creating the rocket by molding an egg-shaped ball of strengthened red fondant into an elongated cone shape. Moisten the end of a cake-pop stick and press into the base. This will support the rocket above the cake. While the fondant is still slightly soft, use the back of a knife to emboss three lines from the point of the rocket down to the base.

7 Mold a base to fit the bottom of the rocket from a small ball of strengthened blue fondant. Moisten the surface with a little water and slip it onto the cake-pop stick so that it sits firmly against the red body. Roll out a thin rope of blue fondant and affix around the top of the blue base with a little water, smoothing the seam with your finger.

8 Roll out a little strengthened gray fondant to $^1/_{16}$in (2mm) thick and use the $^3/_4$in (2cm) circular cutter to create a porthole for the rocket. Use the piping tip to emboss the surface with tiny circles around the perimeter. Let dry, ideally overnight.

9 Mold three pea-sized balls of gray fondant to form the exhausts. Let dry, ideally overnight. Once dry, spray them with silver luster until evenly covered—place the porthole and exhausts on a sheet of newspaper or parchment paper while spraying to keep the work surface clean.

10 Attach the silver exhausts to the bottom of the rocket with a little royal icing. Roll a small amount of strengthened red fondant to ¹/₁₆in (2mm) thick and cut four curved fins, using a sharp knife. Let dry overnight. Once hard, attach to the base of the rocket using a little royal icing.

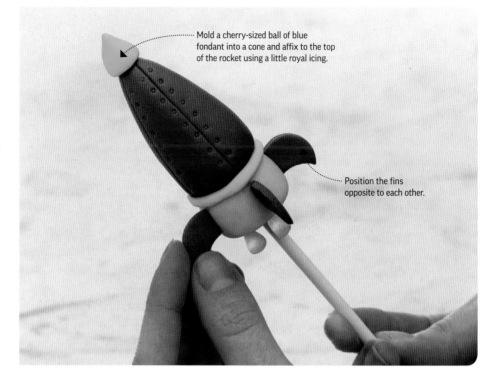

Mold a cherry-sized ball of blue fondant into a cone and affix to the top of the rocket using a little royal icing.

Position the fins opposite to each other.

11 Dust a surface with cornstarch. Roll out red, yellow, and orange fondant to ¹/₁₆in (2mm) thick and cut out flame shapes using a sharp knife. Allow to dry for 1–2 days, until firm. Moisten the back of the silver porthole, and press onto the front of the rocket. Attach the flames beneath the exhausts with a little royal icing, once they are dry and completely hard.

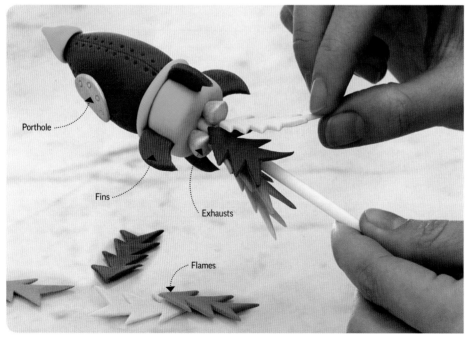

Porthole

Fins

Exhausts

Flames

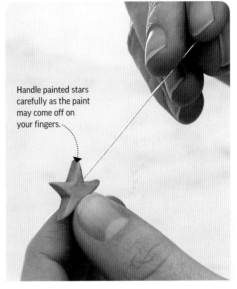

Handle painted stars carefully as the paint may come off on your fingers.

12 Dust a surface with cornstarch. Roll out the yellow fondant to about $^1/_{16}$in (2mm) thick. Use the star cutter to create 25 stars. Paint all 25 stars with the gold dust mix, or place them on a sheet of newspaper or parchment paper and spray with gold luster spray. When dry, turn over and paint the other side. Let the stars dry for at least 1 hour.

13 Gently insert one silver wire each into 10 of the golden stars, moistening the end of the wire to secure. Let dry overnight.

Silver dragées add shimmer to the covered cake drum.

14 Place the unwired stars in the pre-cut star shapes on the cake drum. Use a dot of royal icing, or apply a little water with a fine paintbrush to the silver dragées, and dot them randomly around the covered cake drum, pressing gently into the fondant surface. Secure the black ribbon around the drum with a little craft glue, and set aside to harden.

15 Place the dome cake on the drum. Using a palette knife, paddle the buttercream onto the cake to create an "ombre" effect, with one half of the dome light gray and the other half dark gray. Blend in the middle to create a blurred line where the 2 shades merge. Aim for a rippled, uneven surface.

16 Dust a surface with cornstarch. Roll out the remaining black fondant to $^1/_{16}$in (2mm) thick, and use the circular cutters to cut out 10–12 circles of varying sizes. Press these into the surface of the buttercream, in a random pattern, to form craters. Let dry.

17 Move the aliens onto the craters on the surface of the cake, moistening their bases with a little water or royal icing to glue in place. Twist the wires of the wired stars together to create an uneven spray. Poke the ends of the wired stars into a flower pick, and insert into the cake, so none of the pick is showing.

18 Insert the finished rocket into the cake, allowing it to hover over the surface on the cake-pop stick, as if blasting off, and display.

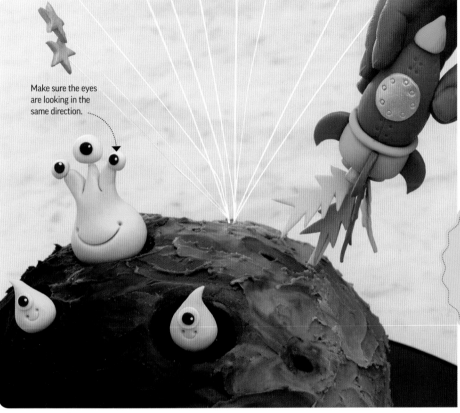

Make sure the eyes are looking in the same direction.

Flames

You can replace strengthened fondant with flower paste—it dries harder and can be rolled out very thinly. Roll out on vegetable shortening instead of cornstarch.

Roll out a rope of white fondant, flatten slightly, and affix with water.

Planet Cake Pops

Create planet cake pops for party favors or to accessorize your cake. Insert sticks into nine cake pops and allow to set. Dip each cake pop in one color of melted candy melt, allow to harden, and then dip it and twirl again in a second color, to create a marbled effect.

Use these color combinations: orange and white for Mercury, green and yellow for Venus, blue and green for Earth, red and orange for Mars, red and white for Jupiter, pearl white for Saturn, pale blue for Uranus, purple and blue for Neptune, and white and blue for dwarf planet Pluto.

Furry Teddy Bear

This delightful cake is the perfect centerpiece for any child's party, and is easily made using a ball cake stacked on top of carved sponge cakes. Support your furry friend with dowels and create a soft pink fondant bow to complete this cheerful teddy bear.

 PREP 1 hr    **BAKE** 40 mins    **DECORATE** 2–3 hrs, plus overnight drying time   **SERVES** 40

Ingredients

- cornstarch, for dusting
- 1lb 10oz (750g) pink fondant (see p176)
- 1lb 2oz (500g) cream fondant
- 2 x 4in (10cm) hemisphere sponge cakes (see p 186) sandwiched with vanilla buttercream frosting and crumb coated to create a ball (see p171)
- 2 x 6in (15cm) round sponge cakes stacked and sandwiched with buttercream frosting
- 1 x 5in (12.5cm) hemisphere cake
- 1½ cups (1lb 2oz/500g) vanilla buttercream frosting (see p180)
- confectioner's sugar, for dusting
- 3lb 3oz (1.5kg) light-brown fondant
- 2 tbsp royal icing (see p181)
- 1oz (25g) black fondant
- 1oz (25g) brown fondant

Equipment

- fondant roller and smoother
- 12in (30cm) cake drum
- 1½in (4cm) circular cutter
- palette knife and serrated knife
- 6in (15cm) and 2in (5cm) cake boards
- wheel and ball tools
- 4 plastic dowels
- ribbon cutter, straight sides
- 3¼ft (1m) pink satin ribbon, ½in (1cm) wide
- craft glue

The fondant should be large enough to cover the surface of the drum.

1 Dust a surface with cornstarch and roll out some of the pink fondant to ⅛in (4mm) thick. Brush the cake drum with a little water and lift the fondant onto the drum, smoothing with the fondant smoother. Use the circular cutter to cut out a series of circles from the surface and edges and carefully remove using the palette knife or the cutter. Discard the cut-out circles.

2 Roll out some of the cream fondant to the same thickness as the pink fondant in step 1, and, using the same circular cutter, cut out enough circles to fill the empty spaces on the drum. Allow to set for 1 hour, and then carefully place into the circles to create a polka-dot effect. Gently smooth with the fondant smoother and let harden overnight.

Furry Teddy Bear 43

3 Freeze the stacked, sandwiched cakes for 1 hour. Remove from the freezer and place on the 6in (15cm) cake board. Use a serrated knife to carve the cake into the shape of a torso, discarding any excess cake.

4 Place the sandwiched hemisphere cake (ball) on the 2in (5cm) cake board. Using the palette knife, carefully frost the surface of both cakes with buttercream frosting and smooth (see pp182–183). Refrigerate both the cakes for 1 hour, until they set.

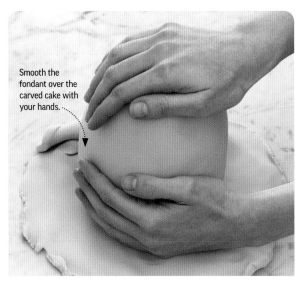

Smooth the fondant over the carved cake with your hands.

5 Dust a surface with confectioner's sugar and roll out half the light-brown fondant to ¼in (5mm) thick, so that it is large enough to cover the carved cake. Lift over the cake and smooth. Cut off the excess fondant and tuck the edges under it. Repeat with the ball cake, tucking the edges under the board. Let set overnight.

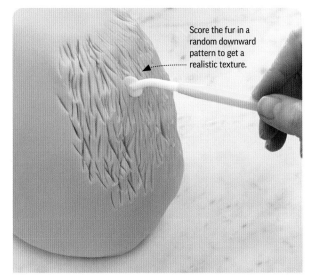

Score the fur in a random downward pattern to get a realistic texture.

6 Use the wheel tool to score the surface of the fondant, covering the torso to create the appearance of fur. Score short and long impressions in a downward direction until the whole surface is covered. Next, score the surface of the ball cake, which will form the head.

Dowels help the torso to support the head.

7 Once set, insert one dowel into the center of the torso and cut it so that it is flush with the surface. Repeat with two more dowels so that the torso of the teddy bear is stable.

8 Place the iced ball cake on top of the bowl cake, affixing in place using royal icing. Hold until secure and let set for 2–3 hours.

9 While the body is setting, strengthen most of the remaining light-brown fondant (see p176) and roll four sausages to create the arms and legs. Round off both ends of each arm and then use the fondant roller to flatten one end of each, where the arm will be affixed to the torso.

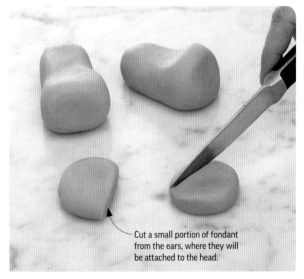

Cut a small portion of fondant from the ears, where they will be attached to the head.

10 From the remaining two sausages, model two legs with a flat bottom for the feet. Cut the other ends into a soft diagonal, where they will be affixed to the base of the torso. Model the remaining fondant into two balls and flatten to create ears.

Furry Teddy Bear 45

11 Use the wheel tool to score the surface of the arms, legs, and ears to create the appearance of fur, in the same way as the head and torso.

12 Dust a surface with confectioner's sugar and roll out some of the remaining cream fondant to ¼in (5mm) thick and cut out an oval to form the belly. Cut a smaller oval from the same sheet of fondant to form the muzzle.

13 Move the bear's body to the center of the covered cake drum, using a little royal icing to secure. Affix the belly and muzzle in place with a little water or royal icing and finish with the fondant smoother. Use the back of a knife and a circular cutter to score a smile.

Push the ball tool into the sockets lightly to create the eyes.

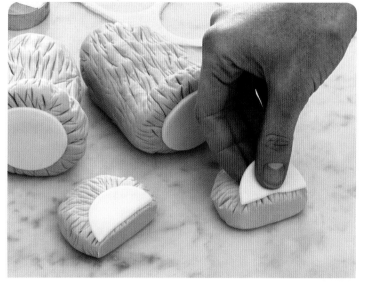

14 Use the ball tool to press two eye sockets into the head. Roll two small balls of strengthened black fondant and push into the sockets, fixing them in place with water. To make the nose, model the brown fondant into a soft triangle, fixing it into place at the top of the oval muzzle with a little water.

15 Dust a surface with confectioner's sugar and roll out the remaining cream fondant to $^1/_{16}$–$^1/_8$in (2–3mm) thick. Using the circular cutter, cut three circles. Use two circles for the feet and cut the remaining circle into half to get two semicircles for the ears. Affix in place with a little water or royal icing and finish with the fondant smoother.

16 When the fondant limbs and body have set, apply royal icing to the inside of the arms and carefully affix them to the sides of the torso. Hold them in place with your fingers until set. To affix the legs, apply royal icing to the diagonal end of the legs. Carefully lift each leg using a palette knife and attach to the torso, holding it in place until set.

Royal icing can also be used to create the sparkle in the eyes.

17 Roll two tiny dots of cream fondant and affix to the eyes with a little water, to create a sparkle. To attach the ears on the teddy bear, apply a little royal icing to the cut edge of each ear and place on the head. Hold the ears in place with your fingers until firm.

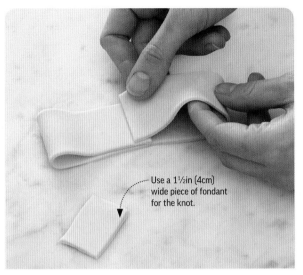

Use a 1¹⁄₂in (4cm) wide piece of fondant for the knot.

18 To create the bow, dust a surface with confectioner's sugar and roll out the remaining pink fondant to ¹⁄₈in (3mm) thick. Use the ribbon cutter to cut four strips of ribbon —three 1in (2.5cm) wide and one 1¹⁄₂in (4cm) wide—all about 6in (15cm) long. Fold over the wider ribbon and place the edges one over the other at the center. Affix using a little water.

Use the wheel tool to score lines on the bow for a gathered effect.

19 Pinch the bow at the center so the fondant sets into soft folds. Wrap the 1¹⁄₂in (4cm) fondant strip around the center of the bow, and secure with a little water. Score with the wheel tool and let dry for about 2 hours.

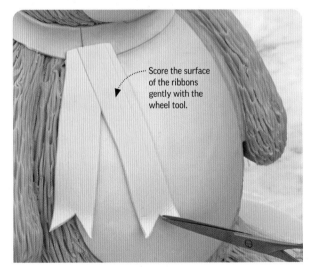

Score the surface of the ribbons gently with the wheel tool.

20 Affix one of the ribbons around the neck with water or royal icing, with the join at the front. Affix the other two ribbons together, curling them up slightly at the bottom to the center of the collar of the teddy bear. Snip a small triangle from the bottom of both the ribbons.

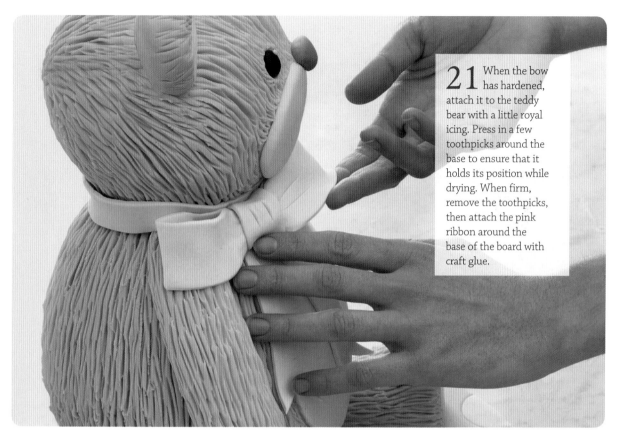

21 When the bow has hardened, attach it to the teddy bear with a little royal icing. Press in a few toothpicks around the base to ensure that it holds its position while drying. When firm, remove the toothpicks, then attach the pink ribbon around the base of the board with craft glue.

Paw-print Cupcakes

Serve these gorgeous paw-print cupcakes alongside the cake or send them home with your party guests. Lightly frost the surface of cooled cupcakes (see pp174–175) with a little buttercream frosting using a palette knife. Dust a surface with confectioner's sugar and roll out white fondant. Use a circular cutter to create tops for the cupcakes—they should be just big enough to cover the surface of your cupcakes. Moisten the backs of the tops with a little water and affix to the cupcakes, smoothing with the fondant smoother. On a dusted surface, roll out the light-brown and pink fondants to about $1/8$in (3mm) thick, and use circular cutters to cut three small circles and one large circle for each cupcake. Affix with a little water.

Treasure Island

With its realistic sugar sand, scary shark, cute crab, and treasure chest stuffed with candies, this cake is bound to be a hit with pirate fans. The chest is made with chocolate finger cookies and its contents can be hand-selected. Add pirate cake pops and cupcakes to create the perfect display.

PREP 1hr   **BAKE** 25–30 mins   **DECORATE** 4–5 hrs, plus overnight drying time   **SERVES** 20

Ingredients

- 1¾oz (50g) dark-brown fondant, strengthened
- cornstarch, for dusting
- 2½oz (75g) green flower paste (see p177)
- 3½oz (100g) gray fondant, strengthened
- ¾oz (20g) each white, black, and orange fondant, strengthened
- dry spaghetti
- 2 cups royal icing, tinted sea blue, plus extra tinted green (see p181)
- 2 x 8in (20cm) square vanilla sponge cakes (see p164), sandwiched with buttercream frosting (see p171)
- ¾ cup (9oz/250g) buttercream frosting (see p180)
- 1 cup light brown sugar
- confectioner's sugar, for dusting
- 7oz (200g) green fondant, strengthened (see p176)
- 7oz (200g) dark chocolate, melted
- 20 chocolate cookie fingers
- 3½oz (100g) yellow fondant, strengthened
- edible gold luster dust, plus superwhite dust (optional)
- grain alcohol
- ¼ cup white royal icing
- mixed assorted candies

continued on the next page...

Snip in an uneven pattern so that it resembles the bark of a coconut tree.

1 Begin by making the tree. Mold a sausage of dark-brown fondant around a cake-pop stick, so that it tapers at the top. Use scissors to snip upside-down V-shapes into the surface, to create the impression of bark. Let dry overnight.

2 Dust a surface with cornstarch and roll out the green flower paste to ¹⁄₁₆in (2mm) thick. Use a sharp knife to cut out 6–10 leaves. Lightly score the surface using the wheel tool. To make coconuts, roll three cherry-sized balls of the dark-brown fondant and shape into ovals. Let dry overnight.

Equipment

- cake-pop stick, plus one stick extra (optional)
- small circular cutter
- fondant roller
- sharp knife
- wheel tool
- artists' paintbrush
- cocktail stick
- ball tool
- small circular cutter
- serrated knife
- 12in (30cm) square cake drum
- palette knife
- small sewing or nail scissors
- 3 small piping cones
- pirate flag, for decoration
- 3¼ft (1m) gray satin ribbon, ½in (1cm) wide
- craft glue

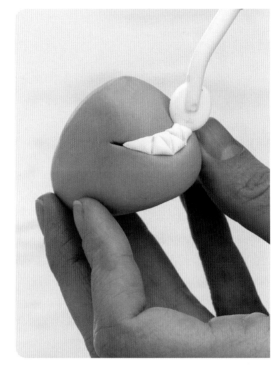

3 To make the shark, model a little of the gray fondant into a blunt cone. Cut out a wedge from the broad side for the mouth, and then smooth the edges to form a soft curve. Fit a wedge of white fondant into the mouth, attaching with water, and score teeth into the surface with the wheel tool.

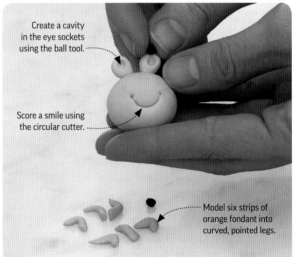

Create a cavity in the eye sockets using the ball tool.

Score a smile using the circular cutter.

Model six strips of orange fondant into curved, pointed legs.

4 Roll out the remaining gray fondant to ¹/₁₆in (2mm) thick and use a sharp knife to cut four gently curved fins. Poke the end of a paintbrush into the face of the shark for eye sockets, and fill with tiny balls of black fondant. Using a toothpick, poke two holes for the nostrils. Set it all aside to dry overnight.

5 For the crab, roll a cherry-sized ball of orange fondant for the head. Roll two tiny balls of the same fondant and flatten a little for eyes. Create eye sockets with the ball tool and affix two tiny balls of black fondant into the cavities with water. Make six pointed legs and attach to the body with water.

 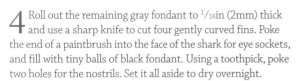

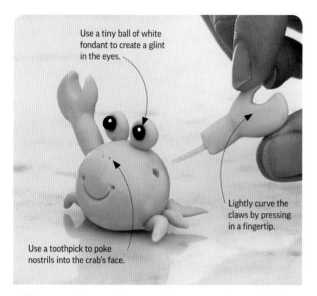

Use a tiny ball of white fondant to create a glint in the eyes.

Lightly curve the claws by pressing in a fingertip.

Use a toothpick to poke nostrils into the crab's face.

Make sure the leaves overlap at the tips to form a strong base.

6 To create claws, make two small sausages of orange fondant, each on a small piece of dry spaghetti. Model a small ball at the end of each, flatten with the roller, then snip out a V-shape on each using scissors. Let harden for 1 hour, then affix to the body using the spaghetti. Set aside to dry overnight.

7 Assemble the tree by fixing the coconuts and leaves together with the green royal icing. Hold each leaf in place, or support with folded kitchen towel, until the royal icing just begins to set.

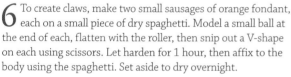

8 Carefully place the trunk in the center of the leaves and affix with the green royal icing. Hold with your fingers until firm. Let dry for 2–3 hours.

9 Freeze the sandwiched sponge cakes for 1 hour. Remove from the freezer, place on parchment paper, and carve into a rugged island shape using a serrated knife. Discard the trimmings and crumb coat the cake with buttercream frosting (see p171), then refrigerate for 30 minutes.

Score lines around the edges
using the wheel tool. ········

10 Carefully lift the cake onto the cake drum, then apply a second coating of buttercream frosting using the palette knife. Press the brown sugar into the buttercream so it covers the top and sides, giving the impression of sand. Allow to set for 30 minutes then brush away any excess sugar from the drum.

11 Dust a surface with confectioner's sugar, and roll out the green fondant to about ¹/₈in (3mm) thick. Using a sharp knife, cut an irregular rectangle to cover the top of the island. Attach with water, then shape the edges into uneven scallops. Refrigerate the island until all the other cake elements are ready.

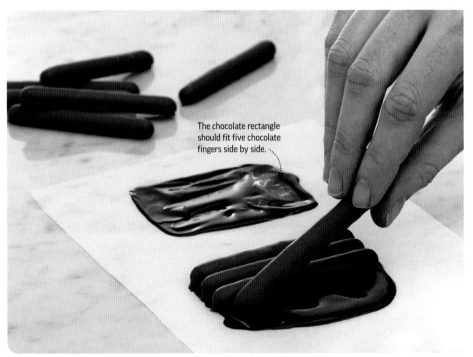
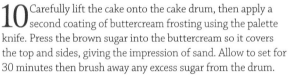

The chocolate rectangle
should fit five chocolate
fingers side by side. ·····

12 For the treasure chest, brush a rectangle of melted chocolate onto parchment paper. Place five chocolate fingers on the melted chocolate. Let harden and remove from the parchment paper. Repeat to create three more panels. Use a sharp knife to cut off any excess chocolate.

13 Cut one panel in half to create the sides of the chest. Fill a piping cone with melted chocolate. Apply a little chocolate to the edges of the panel to assemble the chest. Set aside one panel for the lid.

Apply melted chocolate to the half panels to attach to the sides of the chest.

Piping cone

Fold a square of parchment paper in half to make a triangle, then in half again. Roll it over into a cone shape, and expand it out with your fingers. Fill with chocolate and snip off the end.

Fold each rectangle in an L-shape and attach to the edges of the chest.

14 Roll out the yellow fondant to about ¹⁄₁₆in (2mm) thick, and cut four rectangles. Create rivets in the rectangles with the end of a paintbrush, as shown, then affix to the chest with a little water. Mix the edible gold luster dust with grain alcohol and paint the rectangles. Let dry.

15 Use a palette knife to paddle the blue royal icing over the surface of the cake drum, around the island, to create a series of waves, ensuring that the surface of the drum is covered. Smooth waves up the side of the island. Set for 30 minutes.

16 Pipe white royal icing to the tips of the waves in a series of squiggles to create whitecaps. Sprinkle a little brown sugar around the base of the island to create a beach effect.

17 Press the head of the shark into the royal-icing sea and place a fin directly behind it. Affix the remaining fins into the royal-icing sea around the base of the island.

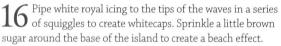

Assembling

You can use green candy melts instead of royal icing to attach the leaves and trunk. Simply melt and apply with a paintbrush. Let harden before placing the tree on the island.

18 Set the treasure chest on top of the island. Press the tree onto the top of the cake so that the cake-pop stick supports it.

Pipe some melted chocolate to attach the half-open lid and hold until firm.

19 Place the crab on the cake, attaching with a little water. Fill the treasure chest with candies, such as, candy necklaces, gold coins, candy-coated chocolate buttons, and jelly beans, so they spill over the sides. Add a jaunty store-bought pirate flag to the top of the chest. Finally, attach the ribbon around the base of the drum with craft glue.

Cake-pop Pirates

Dip cake pops into ivory or flesh-colored candy melts (see p173), or white chocolate, if desired. Allow to set, and melt red, green, and blue candy melts in separate bowls. Dip just the tops of the balls into the melts to create bandanas. Model ties from red, green, and blue fondant, and attach with a little water. Use an edible black pen to create eyes, a smile, and the stubble.

To make the nose, roll a tiny ball of flesh-colored fondant and affix to the face with water. Roll out black fondant very thinly and cut out eye patches, attaching onto the face with water. To finish, tie matching lengths of colored ribbons at the base of each cake pop.

Easy *animal* cakes

Simple round sponge cakes can be transformed into a virtual zoo of animals. Bake two cakes, one for the face and one to make extra legs, snouts and ears. Add colored buttercream frosting, some store-bought goodies, and a little imagination for an impressive party cake. You could use any leftover cake to make some animal cake pops.

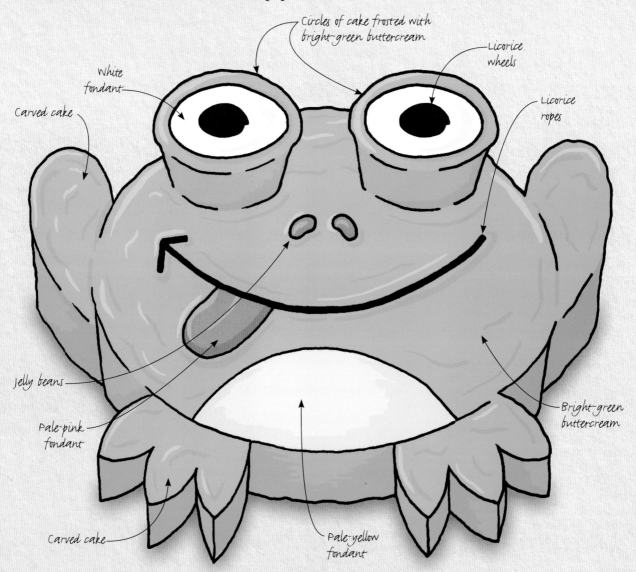

Circles of cake frosted with bright-green buttercream

Licorice wheels

White fondant

Licorice ropes

Carved cake

Bright-green buttercream

Jelly beans

Pale-pink fondant

Carved cake

Pale-yellow fondant

Friendly frog

Playful panda

Natural buttercream

Black buttercream

Carved cake

Black gummy candies

Carved cake

Strawberry licorice ropes

Black buttercream

Black fondant

Black fondant

Bright-orange buttercream

Natural buttercream

Carved cake

Pink jelly beans

Black licorice laces

Pale-pink fondant

White marshmllows, halved, with green diamond gummy candy

Tame tiger

Chocolate buttercream

Pale-yellow fondant

Light chocolate buttercream

Carved cake

Light chocolate buttercream

Melted milk chocolate, piped

Giant chocolate buttons

**Mischievous
monkey**

Pink fondant triangles

Black licorice

Pink fondant

Circle of cake

Pink fondant

Bright-pink candy melts, piped

Black gummy candies

Pretty pig

Over the Rainbow

Create this stunning rainbow cake from multicolored layers of sponge cake, frosted with matching rows of buttercream frosting. Place a gorgeous fondant rainbow, dusted with glitter and sitting on fluffy clouds, on top to create a perfect party centerpiece.

 PREP 1½ hrs   **BAKE** 1½ hrs   **DECORATE** 2–3 hrs, plus overnight drying time   **SERVES** 20-25

Ingredients

- 1oz (25g) lilac fondant, strengthened (see p176)
- 1oz (25g) light-blue fondant, strengthened
- 1½oz (45g) light-green fondant, strengthened
- 1½oz (45g) yellow fondant, strengthened
- 1½oz (45g) orange fondant, strengthened
- 1½oz (45g) fuchsia fondant, strengthened
- cornstarch, for dusting
- 14oz (400g) white fondant, strengthened
- 2 batches of vanilla sponge cake batter (see p164)
- 1¼ tsp lilac food coloring paste
- 1¼ tsp turquoise food coloring paste
- 1¼ tsp light-green food coloring paste
- 1¼ tsp yellow food coloring paste
- 1¼ tsp orange food coloring paste
- 1¼ tsp pink food coloring paste
- 4 cups (2lb 2oz/1kg) vanilla buttercream frosting (see p180)
- fine edible glitter

continued on the next page...

1 To make the rainbow topper, roll each of the six colors of fondant into ropes, about ¼in (5mm) wide and 6in (15cm) long. On a dusted surface, place the circular cutter, or a wide-based glass, and position the lilac rope around it in the shape of a rainbow. Brush the outside edge of the rope with a little water and carefully press the blue rope around it. Continue with all the colors, until all ropes are in position.

2 While the fondant ropes are still soft, use the sharp knife to cut the rainbow evenly across the ends, to give it a flat base. Let to dry for 2 days.

Equipment

- 2½in (6cm) circular cutter
- sharp knife
- fondant roller
- 12in (30cm) cake drum
- fondant smoother
- two 8in (20cm) round cake pans
- palette knife
- large piping bag
- large round piping tip (such as Wilton no. 1A)
- 3¼ft (1m) pink satin ribbon, ½in (1cm) wide
- craft glue

3 Dust a surface with cornstarch. Using the fondant roller, roll out the strengthened white fondant to about ¹⁄₈in (3mm) thick. It should be large enough to cover the cake drum. Brush the cake drum with a little water and cover with the fondant, using the smoother to create an even surface (see p179). Trim the excess fondant using a sharp knife and wrap in plastic wrap for later use. Let dry overnight.

Trim off any excess fondant to give the clouds a neat finish.

4 To make the clouds, mold some of the reserved white fondant into 30 small balls, each approximately the size of a small marble, and set aside to harden for 3 hours.

5 On a dusted surface, roll out the rest of the reserved white fondant into a very thin sheet. Cut into two and press each half over 15 balls. Trim the excess and tuck the edges under the clouds. Set aside for 3 hours.

Cool the cakes in the pans for 10 minutes, then turn them onto a wire rack.

6 Prepare the baking pans (see pp168–9). Divide the batter between six bowls, add 1 teaspoon of food coloring paste to each, and blend, to get lilac, turquoise, green, yellow, orange, and pink batters. Bake for 25 minutes and let cool. Trim off any brown edges and level the cakes (see pp170–1).

7 Divide the buttercream frosting into seven bowls and tint six using one of each food coloring paste (see p180). Start with the lilac cake and top with lilac buttercream frosting. Place the turquoise cake on top and smooth turquoise frosting over it. Top with the green cake and a layer of green frosting.

Use a palette knife to smooth the pale turquoise buttercream frosting.

8 Continue stacking the cakes with their corresponding buttercream frosting colors, following the image on page 60, until you finish with the pink sponge cake on top. Move the cake to the covered cake drum.

9 Crumb coat the entire cake (see p171) using the untinted buttercream frosting, and refrigerate for 30–60 minutes. Add some of the untinted frosting to the leftover turquoise frosting and smooth over the top of the cake. Let set for 1 hour.

Over the Rainbow 63

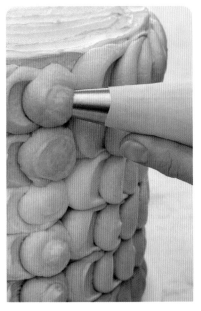

10 Attach the piping tip to the piping bag and fill with lilac buttercream frosting. Carefully pipe a large dot of buttercream frosting onto the lilac layer of the cake.

11 Dip the palette knife in a bowl of warm water and press into the dot to create a scallop. Repeat until you have created a row around the entire cake.

12 Continue with the turquoise, green, yellow, orange, and pink frosting, until the whole cake is covered. Finish each row with a large dot, and then let set for 1–1½ hours.

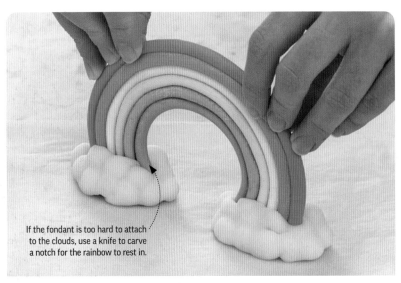

If the fondant is too hard to attach to the clouds, use a knife to carve a notch for the rainbow to rest in.

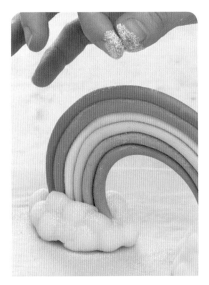

13 Attach the clouds to each end of the rainbow, using a little water to affix. Let dry, until it is hard and firm enough to stand upright.

14 Once the rainbow and clouds have dried, lightly dust the surface with edible glitter to add some sparkle.

15 Apply a little water at the base of the clouds and carefully position the rainbow and clouds on top of the cake. Let set for 1 hour, then affix the ribbon in place around the base of the covered cake drum, using craft glue.

Pop of Color Cupcakes

Simple cupcakes (see pp174–3), frosted with pastel buttercream frosting to match the colors of the rainbow, are a perfect addition to your party table. Pile buttercream frosting onto the center of each cupcake and use a palette knife to spread the frosting in a generous swirl, working from the inside out. If desired, you can make mini rainbows or clouds from leftover fondant. If you lay them flat on the cupcakes, they won't need to harden first.

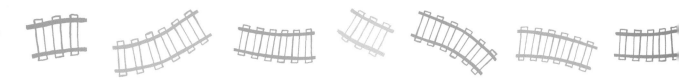

Party Train

Load this colorful, three-dimensional train with sweet cargo, and set it on edible train tracks, complete with ballast. Easily carved from sponge cakes, and using store-bought decorations, it is a show-stopper cake that will charm any child.

PREP 1 hr   **BAKE** 40-50 mins   **DECORATE** 2½-3 hrs, plus overnight drying time   **SERVES** 20

Ingredients

- cornstarch, for dusting
- 1lb 2oz (500g) green fondant, strengthened (see p186)
- 2 x 9in (23cm) square sponge cakes (see p186)
- 1½ cups (1lb 2oz/500g) vanilla buttercream (see p180)
- confectioner's sugar, for dusting
- 10oz (300g) blue fondant
- 10oz (300g) red fondant
- miniature and full-sized chocolate sandwich cookies
- ¼ cup royal icing (see p181)
- mixed candies, including candy-coated chocolate buttons and jelly beans
- 1 miniature cupcake
- 1 large marshmallow

continued on the next page...

Candy-covered chocolate buttons make perfect accessories for the engine and cars.

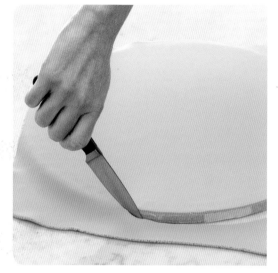

1 Dust a surface with cornstarch and roll out the strengthened green fondant to about ⅛in (3mm) thick. The fondant should be large enough to cover the cake drum. Brush the cake drum with a little water and cover with the fondant, using the fondant smoother to create an even surface. Cut off the excess using a sharp knife. Let the covered drum dry overnight. Wrap the remaining green fondant in plastic wrap and reserve for later use.

2 To create the train cars, cut three rectangular blocks, each about 3¼in x 2in (8cm x 5cm), out of one of the cakes. Place the blocks on a sheet of parchment paper and crumb coat each block with buttercream frosting (see p171). Let set for 1 hour.

- rectangular shortbread-style cookies
- 7oz (200g) dark-gray fondant, strengthened
- 10oz (300g) orange fondant
- 10oz (300g) green fondant
- chocolate finger cookies
- 7oz (200g) light-gray fondant, strengthened
- cotton candy

Equipment

- fondant roller
- 14in (35cm) round cake drum
- fondant smoother
- sharp knife
- palette knife
- small artist's paintbrush
- piping bag
- 1 small round tip (Wilton no. 4)
- 3¼ft (1m) blue satin ribbon, ½ in (1cm) wide
- craft glue

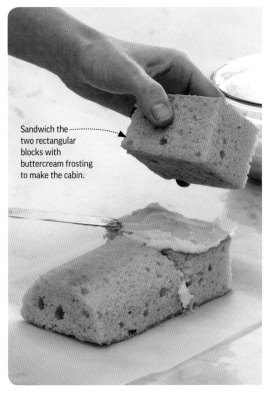

Sandwich the two rectangular blocks with buttercream frosting to make the cabin.

3 To make the engine, cut out two rectangular blocks from the other sponge cake, each about 3¼in x 2½in (8cm x 6cm). Use a sharp knife to carve one of the blocks into a half cylinder to form the front section of the train and place on a sheet of parchment paper. Cut the remaining block in half. Attach one half to the front of the train with buttercream frosting. Spread buttercream frosting on top and place the second half on top. Crumb coat the whole engine with buttercream frosting (see p171). Let set for 1 hour.

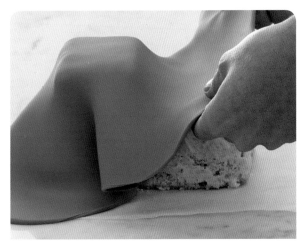

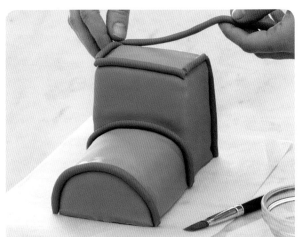

4 Lightly frost the surface of the engine with buttercream. Dust a surface with confectioner's sugar and roll out the blue fondant to ⅛in (3mm) thick. Cover the engine with the fondant, smoothing it with your hands, or use the smoother. Cut away the excess and tuck the edges underneath.

5 Roll several long, narrow ropes of some of the red fondant, about ¼in (5mm) thick. From these, cut smaller ropes to "pipe" the top of the cabin and the front of the engine. Moisten the backs of the ropes with water using a paintbrush and affix into place on the train.

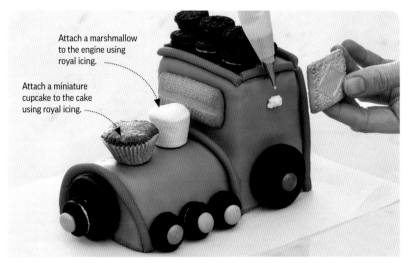

Attach a marshmallow to the engine using royal icing.

Attach a miniature cupcake to the cake using royal icing.

6 Fix miniature chocolate cookies to each side of the engine with royal icing, to create wheels. Affix two large chocolate cookies to make wheels for the cabin. Attach another large chocolate cookie to the front of the train and top with a smaller one. Stick a candy-coated chocolate button to each wheel using royal icing. Glue miniature chocolate cookies to the top of the cabin, using royal icing. Fit four shortcake-style cookies to the front, back, and sides of the cabin, to create windows.

7 Using the strengthened dark-gray fondant, roll tiny balls to create the stones for the ballast. Let harden for about 5 hours.

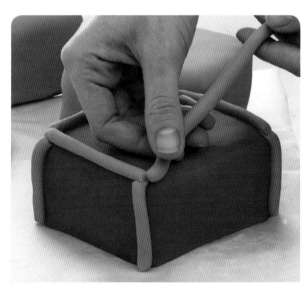

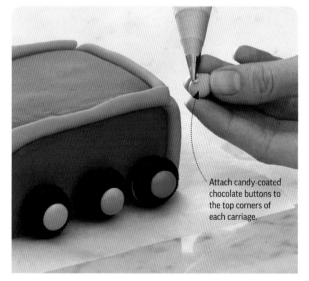

Attach candy-coated chocolate buttons to the top corners of each carriage.

8 Cover the three cars using the red, orange, and green fondant, as in step 4. Create borders for the cars, rolling orange ropes to pipe the red car, blue ropes for the green car, and green ropes for the orange car. Attach the fondant ropes with water.

9 Add miniature chocolate cookies to create wheels on the sides, and top each with a candy-coated chocolate button. Add another to the front of each car, to create a headlight, attaching all with royal icing.

Using a sharp knife, cut out ¼in (5mm) wide ribbons.

10 Apply a thin layer of royal icing, or edible glue, on top of each carriage. Fill the top of the orange car with jelly beans, the green car with chocolate finger cookies, and the red car with candy-coated chocolate buttons—or choose your own "cargo." Place the engine and the cars on the covered cake drum in a semicircle.

11 For the tracks, dust a surface with cornstarch and roll out the light-gray fondant to ¹⁄₁₆in (2mm) thick. Cut out long ribbons to fit between the cars and the engine, and from the ends of the train to the edge of the drum.

12 Moisten the backs of the ribbons with water and smooth into place on the cake drum, so that they form a gentle curve. Use the end of the piping tip to emboss rivets on them.

13 Attach the chocolate finger cookies between the tracks, using a little royal icing, for ties. When the stones are dry, dab the spaces between the finger cookies with royal icing and fill with the stones.

14 Let the cake set for 1 hour, and then affix the blue ribbon around the base of the drum using craft glue.

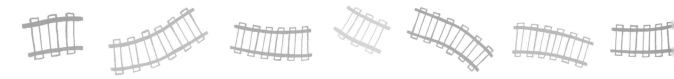

15 Pipe a peak of buttercream frosting on the miniature cupcake and let dry. Finally, press a puff of cotton candy steam into the buttercream frosting.

Cargo Cupcakes

Replicate the cargo cars of your train with candy-topped cupcakes (see pp174–5)—perfect for goody bags. Fit a large circular piping tip onto a large piping bag and fill with green buttercream frosting. Pipe a generous swirl onto the surface of each cupcake, and then top with candies to match your cars—or create new cargo altogether.

Animal cake pops

No matter what your theme, an animal cake pop is bound to complete it! Model your cake pops to shape, chill, dip in candy melts, and decorate with a variety of easy-to-find ingredients and easy-to-master coating and piping techniques.

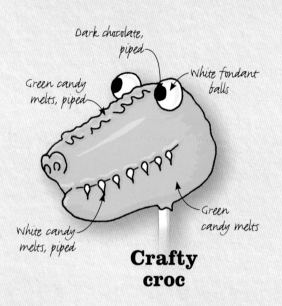

Dark chocolate, piped

White fondant balls

Green candy melts, piped

White candy melts, piped

Green candy melts

Crafty croc

Light-gray candy melts

Dark chocolate, piped

Blue candy-coated chocolate candies

Large heart-shaped sprinkle, inverted

small heart-shaped sprinkle

Flower sprinkles

Cute owl

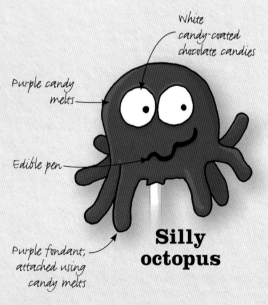

White candy-coated chocolate candies

Purple candy melts

Edible pen

Purple fondant, attached using candy melts

Silly octopus

Fondant cone covered in gold edible glitter

Pink candy melts

White/pale pink fondant

Edible pen

Various colors of food coloring paste, mixed with grain alcohol and painted on

Magic unicorn

Speedy snail

Light-green candy melts

Edible pen

Round mints

Edible pen

Green candy melts

Cuddly koala

Gray fondant disk, attached using candy melts

Black jelly bean

Gray candy melts

Edible pen

Baby dinosaur

Edible pen

Red fondant triangles

Blue candy melts

Playful puppy

White chocolate, piped

Dark chocolate, piped

Golden cookie crumbs

Brown fondant oval

Light-brown candy melt

Pretty pufferfish

Red luster dust

Orange candy melts

Edible pen

White candy melts, piped

Heart-shaped sprinkle, halved

Green glitter on piped green candy melts

Tropical parrot

Edible pen

Yellow fondant, attached using candy melts

White candy melts, piped

Dark orange candy melts

Light orange candy melts

Green candy melts

Red candy melts

Dinosaur Egg

This baby dinosaur, with its spiked and spotted tail, just emerging from his egg, is a crowd-pleaser. The egg is made by stacking delicious sponge cakes and wrapping them in ivory fondant that is then speckled with edible paint. Get ready for some prehistoric fun.

PREP 40-50 mins   **BAKE** 1-2 hrs   **DECORATE** 3-4 hrs, plus overnight drying time   **SERVES** 30

Ingredients

- cornstarch, for dusting
- 1lb 2oz (500g) green fondant, strengthened (see p176)
- 9in (23cm) round sponge cake (see p164)
- 8in (20cm) round sponge cake
- 6in (15cm) hemisphere sponge cake (see p186)
- 1½ cups (1lb 2oz/500g) buttercream frosting (see p180)
- confectioner's sugar, for dusting
- 2¼lb (1kg) ivory fondant
- brown food coloring paste
- grain alcohol
- 10oz (300g) crisp rice bars
- vegetable shortening, for greasing
- 1lb 2oz (500g) orange fondant, strengthened
- 1oz (25g) white fondant

continued on the next page...

Speckled candy-covered chocolate eggs or jelly beans are perfect additions to the theme.

1 Dust a surface with cornstarch and roll out the strengthened green fondant to about ¹⁄₈in (3mm) thick, so that it is large enough to cover the cake drum. Brush the cake drum with a little water and cover with the fondant. Use the smoother to create an even surface. Cut off any excess using a sharp knife. Let the covered drum dry overnight. Wrap the remaining green fondant in plastic wrap for later use.

2 Place the 9in (23cm) sponge cake on a sheet of parchment paper. Using the palette knife, paddle some buttercream frosting on the top and place the 8in (20cm) sponge cake on it. Apply some more buttercream frosting on top of this cake and place the inverted bowl cake over it.

- 1oz (25g) black fondant
- 3½oz (100g) blue fondant, strengthened
- 1oz (25g) chocolate

Equipment

- fondant roller and smoother
- 12in (30cm) cake drum
- sharp knife
- palette knife
- serrated knife
- 1 plastic dowel
- small artist's paintbrush
- ball tool
- 2 cake-pop sticks
- toothpicks
- 3¼ft (1m) orange satin ribbon, ½in (1cm) wide
- craft glue

3 Using the serrated knife, carefully carve the structure from the base of the bowl cake down to the bottom of the largest sponge cake to create a smooth, even surface. Carve just enough to produce a gently curved egg shape. Use a palette knife to crumb coat the entire surface of the egg shape (see p171) and refrigerate for 30–60 minutes, until set.

4 Apply a thin layer of buttercream onto the crumb-coated cake and refrigerate for 1 hour more. When the cake has set, press the dowel through its center to provide support.

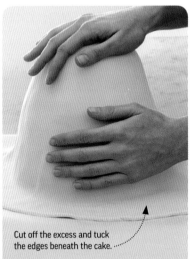

Cut off the excess and tuck the edges beneath the cake.

5 Dust a surface with confectioner's sugar and roll out the ivory fondant to about ⅛in (3mm) thick—it should be large enough to cover the entire cake. Lift the fondant over the cake and smooth down with your hands.

6 Use the sharp knife to score a jagged star shape into the surface of the top side of the cake. Cut out a similar shape at the base of the cake on the opposite side, for the tail to emerge.

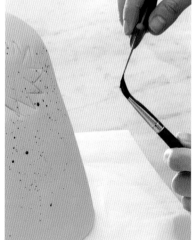

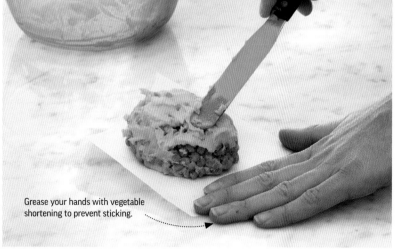

Grease your hands with vegetable shortening to prevent sticking.

7 Mix together the brown food coloring paste and grain alcohol. Dip the paintbrush into it and then flick toward the cake to create a speckled appearance. Set aside, ideally overnight.

8 Model about half the crisp rice bars to form the dinosaur head. Begin by creating a cone shape and then flatten slightly and round the top and bottom. Use your fingers or a ball tool to press in nostrils, eye sockets, and a slight indentation where the snout begins. Place the head on parchment paper, and using the palette knife, or a small spatula, lightly apply some buttercream on it. Let dry.

Press the fondant into the eye sockets and nostrils.

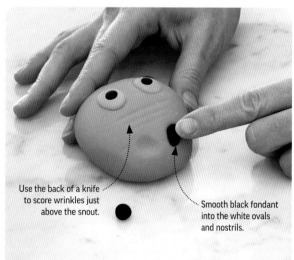

Use the back of a knife to score wrinkles just above the snout.

Smooth black fondant into the white ovals and nostrils.

9 Dust a surface with confectioner's sugar and roll out half of the orange fondant to about 1/8in (3mm) thick. Dust your hands with confectioner's sugar and cover the dinosaur head with fondant. Cut off any excess and tuck the edges under the back of the head, pressing the fondant together with your fingers and then smoothing with the fondant smoother.

10 Model two balls of white fondant, flatten into ovals, and affix into the eye sockets with a little water. Press the ball tool into the white ovals in the center. Roll pea-sized balls of black fondant, moisten the backs, and press into the cavities. Model two slightly larger ovals of black fondant and fit into the nostrils, using a little water. Set aside.

Dinosaur Egg **77**

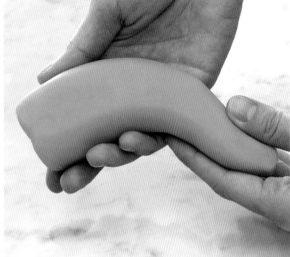

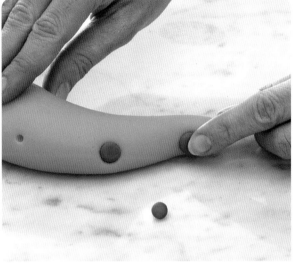

11 Form the remaining crisp rice bars into a gently curved tail—larger at one end and tapering to a point at the other end—about 7in (18cm) in length. Cover with buttercream and then with the orange fondant, as in step 9, using your hands to smooth.

12 While the fondant is still soft, use both ends of the ball tool and the end of the paintbrush to make indentations into the surface of the tail in a random pattern. Model some of the strengthened blue fondant into small balls and carefully press into the cavities, using a little water. Use the fondant smoother to achieve an even surface.

13 Dust a surface with cornstarch and roll out the remaining blue fondant to about ⅛in (3mm) thick. Using a sharp knife cut out 16 spikes (14 the same size, then a larger one for the head and a smaller one for the tip of the tail).

14 Soften the edges of the spikes with your fingers so they are nicely rounded. Moisten the base of each spike with a little water, place the larger spike on the head and the remaining ones down the tail, with the smallest spike at the end.

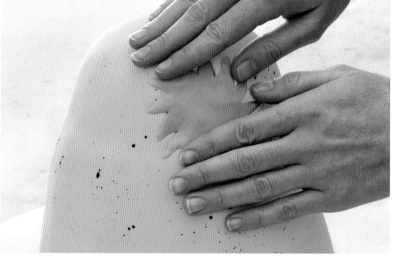

15 Cut out the jagged star shapes from the cake and, using a knife, lift away from the buttercream beneath without pulling away any of the cake. Scrape any buttercream from the back and reserve the star shapes.

16 Dust a surface with confectioner's sugar and roll out the remaining orange fondant to ⅛in (3mm) thick. Use the ivory fondant star shapes as templates to cut two identical shapes from the orange fondant. Moisten the backs and press into the spaces on the cake. Use the ball tool to create some cavities on the surface of each star shape, fill with the blue fondant balls (see step 12), and smooth the surface.

17 Transfer the cake to the covered drum, then press the tail into place against the orange fondant. Use a little water to attach the tail.

Dino head

If you do not feel confident using crisp rice bars for the head and tail, you can make them entirely from fondant. Use cake-pop sticks or dowels to support the head.

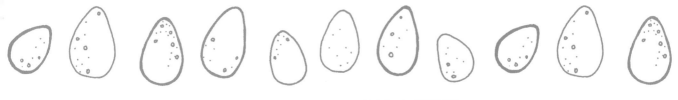

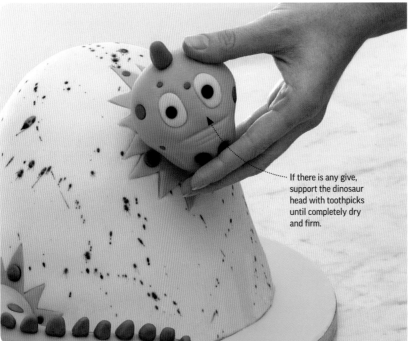

If there is any give, support the dinosaur head with toothpicks until completely dry and firm.

18 Melt the chocolate and dip both ends of each cake-pop stick in it, so about 1in (2.5cm) of each end is covered in chocolate. Press both the sticks down into the cake in the center of the orange broken eggshell shape, about 1¼in (3cm) apart. Make sure that each cake-pop stick protrudes at a slightly upward angle from the surface to support the head fully. Spread a little chocolate on the back of the head, slip the head onto the cake-pop sticks, and press into place. Hold for 2–3 minutes, until the chocolate has hardened.

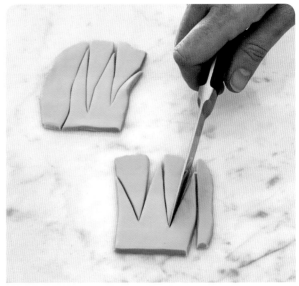

19 Cut out a small jagged star shape from the speckled shape removed from the cake in step 15. Curve over the top right of the dinosaur's head and affix using water.

20 Dust a surface with confectioner's sugar and roll out the remaining green fondant to about ¹⁄₁₆in (2mm) thick. Cut tufts of grass in random heights and shapes. Moisten the backs and affix around the base of the egg.

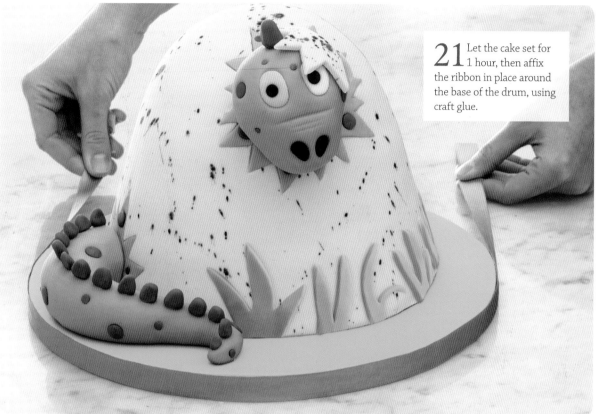

21 Let the cake set for 1 hour, then affix the ribbon in place around the base of the drum, using craft glue.

Dinosuar Egg Cupcakes

These delightful cupcakes are remarkably easy to make. Simply pipe or spread chocolate buttercream frosting or ganache on the surface of each cupcake (see pp174–175), cover with finely grated milk or dark chocolate, and then top with speckled chocolate eggs. These cupcakes would be a great idea for Easter celebrations, too. Add a fondant tail emerging from one of the eggs, if you have the time.

Cupcake Owl

Create this lovely owl by decorating frosted cupcakes with a host of store-bought cookies, chocolates, and candies. It couldn't be easier to make and will delight children with its quirky design. Goody bags spilling over with chocolate "owl eggs" add to the theme.

 PREP 30 mins   **BAKE** 15 mins   **DECORATE** 30-45 mins, plus drying time   **SERVES** 16

Ingredients

- 16 vanilla cupcakes in paper cupcake liners (see p164)
- ²/₃ cup (200g) buttercream frosting, tinted yellow (see p180)
- ³/₄ cup (10oz/300g) buttercream frosting, tinted sage green
- 5 chocolate-covered sponge-cake cookies
- 7oz (200g) white chocolate buttons, reserve one to melt
- 3oz (75g) package of Japanese chocolate-dipped cookie sticks (or pretzels)
- 1oz (25g) milk chocolate, grated
- 3 large milk-chocolate buttons
- 3½oz (100g) chocolate chips

Equipment

- palette knife
- small sharp knife

Chocolate buttons can be made at home with easy-to-use molds.

1 Using the palette knife, cover the surface of six cupcakes with the yellow buttercream frosting. To ensure a smooth surface, dip the knife in warm water before applying the frosting. Cover the remaining 10 cupcakes with the sage-green buttercream frosting. Set them aside.

2 Cut four of the chocolate-covered sponge-cake cookies into halves, and the last cookie into quarters. To make the beak of the owl, take one quarter of the sponge-cake cookie and place it, chocolate-side down, on top of one of the green cupcakes. Place three white chocolate buttons beneath the cookie so that the buttons overlap each other, attaching them using buttercream frosting, if necessary.

3 For the claws, take two quarters of the cookie and cut out inverted V-shapes from each. Place one claw on each of the two yellow cupcakes. Place broken cookie sticks beneath them, to make a branch for the owl to rest on. Cover two more yellow cupcakes with broken cookie sticks.

4 To make the body of the owl, take three green cupcakes and place white-chocolate buttons on them to cover the entire surface. Take two more green cupcakes, cover half of their surface with the white-chocolate buttons, and sprinkle grated milk chocolate on the remaining half of each.

Dot a small amount of melted white chocolate on each eye to create a glint.

5 For the wings, take four green cupcakes and press two halves of the chocolate-covered sponge-cake cookies on one side of each cupcake, overlapping each other. Sprinkle grated chocolate on the remaining portion of each cupcake.

6 For the eyes, place a large milk-chocolate button in the center of the remaining two yellow cupcakes. Surround the perimeter of each cupcake with chocolate chips. Using a sharp knife, cut the last milk-chocolate button in half and press onto the outside edge of each cupcake to create ears.

7 Transfer the decorated cupcakes to a serving plate or board, or directly onto the table. Position the beak, wings, torso, claws, and the branch in four consecutive rows, as shown on page 82.

Little Owlet Cupcakes

Create individual baby owl cupcakes for goody bags by frosting extra cupcakes in yellow or green buttercream and then adding detail. Cut chocolate-covered sponge-cake cookies in half for the wings, and cut smaller V-shapes for the beaks. Create the eyes by topping white-chocolate buttons with chocolate drops and piping on a dot of royal icing. Affix to the cupcakes with a little royal icing. Cut milk-chocolate buttons in half for the ear tufts, and grate chocolate onto the torso. Use buttercream to hold the wings, beak, and ears in position.

In the Jungle

Create a cast of gorgeous jungle animals set in a deep green forest. The sponge cake is frosted with delicious buttercream, with hand-cut leaves, plunger-cutter flowers, twisted vines, and hand-modeled characters. Complement your jungle with a zoo of animal cupcakes.

PREP 1 hr 20 mins **BAKE** 25-30 mins **DECORATE** 4-5 hrs, plus overnight drying time **SERVES** 20-30

Ingredients

- 2 x 8in (20cm) round vanilla sponge cakes (see p164), sandwiched and crumb coated with buttercream frosting (see p171)
- 4½ cups (3lb 3oz/1.5kg) vanilla buttercream frosting, tinted soft green (see p180)
- cornstarch, for dusting
- confectioner's sugar, for dusting
- 1oz (25g) black fondant (see p176)
- dry spaghetti
- 2 tbsp royal icing (see p181)
- 1oz (25g) white fondant, strengthened
- brown food coloring paste
- edible pink dust
- grain alcohol

For the forest
- 7oz (200g) dark-brown fondant, strengthened
- 1lb 2oz (500g) dark-green fondant, strengthened
- 9oz (250g) medium-green fondant, strengthened
- 1¾oz (50g) light-brown fondant, strengthened
- 1oz (25g) orange fondant, strengthened
- 1oz (25g) pink fondant, strengthened

continued on the next page...

1 Place the cake on the cake drum. Using the palette knife, cover the cake with buttercream frosting, spreading it all the way to the edges of the drum. Use a side scraper to achieve a completely smooth surface, or go around the cake with the edge of the palette knife to achieve a smooth finish.

2 To create a grassy texture, use a closed-star piping tip to score the buttercream frosting. Set aside overnight to harden.

Use the knife to cut out branches.

Flatten the branches lightly with the fondant roller.

Score lightly with a knife to create the impression of bark.

3 For the trees, form seven sausages with the dark-brown fondant. They should taper at one end and be tall enough to reach the top of the cake.

- 1oz (25g) yellow fondant, strengthened
- 1oz (25g) purple fondant, strengthened

For the lion
- 2¼oz (65g) light-brown fondant, strengthened
- 1oz (25g) white fondant
- ¼oz (10g) dark-brown fondant, strengthened
- ¾oz (20g) medium-brown fondant, strengthened

For the giraffe
- 3½oz (100g) yellow fondant, strengthened
- ¼oz (10g) dark-brown fondant, strengthened, for the horns
- ¾oz (20g) medium-brown fondant, strengthened

For the snake
- 1¾oz (50g) pale-green fondant, strengthened

For the monkey
- 1¼oz (35g) dark-brown fondant, strengthened
- ¾oz (20g) beige fondant, strengthened

For the elephant
- 2½oz (75g) light-gray fondant, strengthened
- 1oz (25g) flesh-colored fondant, strengthened

Equipment
- palette knife
- 10in (25cm) round cake drum

continued on the next page...

Cut large cloud shapes to form the tops of the trees.

Affix smaller cloud shapes to the branches.

4 Dust a surface with cornstarch, roll out half the dark-green fondant to ⅛in (3mm) thick and use a sharp knife to cut seven large cloud shapes in varying sizes, and about nine smaller cloud shapes. Leave to set for 30 minutes. Roll out the remaining dark-green and half the medium-green fondant. Cut about nine large- and medium-sized clouds from each, cut each in half, and set these aside to dry overnight.

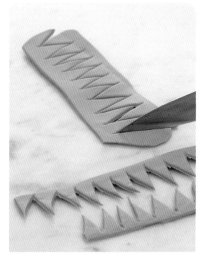

5 To make the vines, dust a surface with confectioner's sugar and roll out eight thin ropes of the light-brown fondant. Score each rope lightly with a knife to create a vinelike effect. Set aside.

6 Roll out the remaining medium-green fondant to ¹⁄₁₆in (2mm) thick, and cut into 30, 3¼–4in (8–10cm) long strips. Using a sharp knife, cut an uneven zigzag pattern throughout to create the appearance of grass.

- side scraper (optional)
- small closed-star piping tip (such as Wilton no. 8)
- sharp knife
- fondant roller
- small blossom plunger cutters
- ball tool
- Dresden tool
- toothpick
- wheel tool
- cake-pop stick
- drinking straw, or modeling tool
- heart-shaped cutter
- ½in (1cm) circular cutters
- small scissors
- small paintbrush
- small round-tip piping tip (such as Wilton no.
- 3¼ft (1m) green satin ribbon, ½in (1cm) wide
- craft glue

7 Roll 20 of the grass strips along the edges to create tufts of grass. Pinch together the ends with a little water to secure.

8 To make the flowers, roll out a little of the orange, pink, yellow, and purple fondants very thinly, and use the plunger cutters to cut 10–12 flowers of each color. Use the ball tool to curve them slightly. Dry for 30 minutes.

9 Affix the trees around the cake at even intervals using a little water. Attach the vines to the cake in swags between the trees and hanging down from the branches. Moisten the bases of the half clouds and press them into the surface of the cake until the top of the cake is covered, so that they rise in an uneven pattern and resemble treetop cover.

Pinch together the points of each blade to shape, as you go.

10 Moisten the back of the remaining strips of grass with water and attach around the base of the cake. Affix the flowers to the cake in a random pattern above the grass line.

11 Moisten the base of each tuft of grass with water and press into the buttercream on the drum. Make sure you leave enough space to place the animals later.

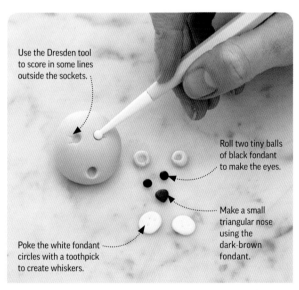

Use the Dresden tool to score in some lines outside the sockets.

Roll two tiny balls of black fondant to make the eyes.

Make a small triangular nose using the dark-brown fondant.

Poke the white fondant circles with a toothpick to create whiskers.

12 For the lion, roll a walnut-sized ball of the light-brown fondant to form the head. Roll two more small balls of the light-brown fondant, flatten them, and pinch them at the base to make ears. Use the smallest end of the ball tool to make the eye sockets and the mouth. Roll out two pea-sized balls of white fondant for the muzzle, flatten, and set aside.

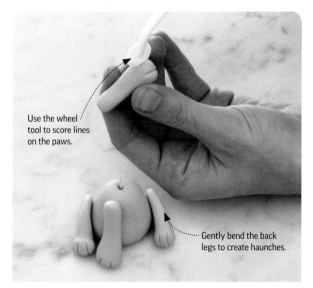

Use the wheel tool to score lines on the paws.

Gently bend the back legs to create haunches.

13 Model a walnut-sized ball of light-brown fondant into a soft egg shape and flatten the bottom. Insert a piece of dry spaghetti into it to attach the head later. Create two front legs from small sausages of fondant with soft round paws that taper up the legs to become narrow at the top. Create a second set for the back legs and affix to the body with water.

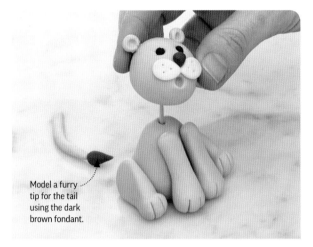

Model a furry tip for the tail using the dark brown fondant.

Place a dot of white fondant on the eyes to create a glint.

14 Place the black fondant eyes into the eye sockets and glue the ears to the head with royal icing. Attach the nose and muzzle to the face, then affix the head to the body on the spaghetti. Use the light-brown fondant to roll a thin tail.

15 Affix the tail to the body with a little water. Roll out a long strip of medium-brown fondant, about $1/16$in (2mm) thick. Use the wheel tool to cut the mane out of it and then score the fur. Set some of the scored fondant aside to use as a tuft of hair.

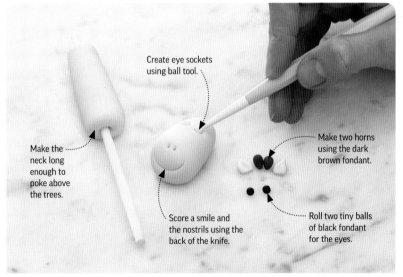

Create eye sockets using ball tool.

Make the neck long enough to poke above the trees.

Score a smile and the nostrils using the back of the knife.

Make two horns using the dark brown fondant.

Roll two tiny balls of black fondant for the eyes.

16 Apply royal icing to the edge of the mane and attach to the head. Roll the leftover fondant strip to form a tuft of mane and affix to the top of the forehead using a little royal icing. Let dry overnight.

17 To make the giraffe, model some of the yellow fondant around a cake-pop stick to form the neck. Leave the other end of the cake-pop stick sticking out of the bottom. Mold a ball of yellow fondant into a gently curved, slightly flattened egg shape for the head. To make the ears, roll out a little yellow fondant, very thinly, and cut two teardrop shapes. Pinch them at the base and affix to the head using a little royal icing.

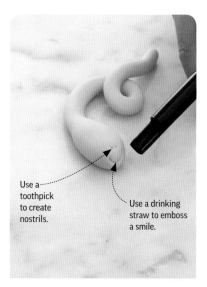

18 Place the eyes into the sockets and affix the ears and horns to the head using royal icing. Attach the head to the neck with royal icing. Create a mane using the medium-brown fondant.

Affix the mane onto the giraffe using water.

19 Place tiny dots of royal icing or white fondant in the eyes to create a glint. Use the edible brown color to paint markings on the giraffe. Let dry overnight.

Mix brown food coloring paste with grain alcohol to create edible paint.

20 To make the snake, roll a sausage of pale-green fondant and use your fingers to mold a head at one end and taper the other end to a point. Curve the body into a spiral.

Use a toothpick to create nostrils.

Use a drinking straw to emboss a smile.

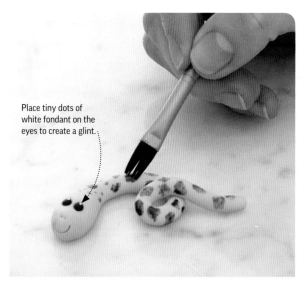

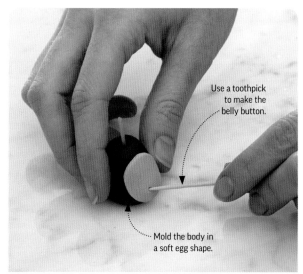

Place tiny dots of white fondant on the eyes to create a glint.

21 To make the eyes, use the ball tool to create sockets and place tiny balls of black fondant into them. Paint on the markings using the edible brown color. Let dry overnight.

Use a toothpick to make the belly button.

Mold the body in a soft egg shape.

22 For the monkey, roll a walnut-sized ball of dark-brown fondant. Insert a piece of dry spaghetti, with enough sticking above the the body to support the head. Dust a surface with cornstarch and roll out some beige fondant thinly. Cut out an oval and attach to the torso, using a little water.

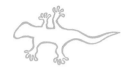

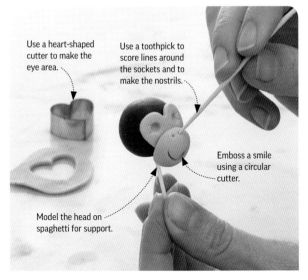

Use a heart-shaped cutter to make the eye area.

Use a toothpick to score lines around the sockets and to make the nostrils.

Emboss a smile using a circular cutter.

Model the head on spaghetti for support.

Roll two tiny balls of black fondant and place into the sockets.

23 For the head, roll a small ball of dark brown fondant. On a dusted surface, roll out some beige fondant and cut out the eye area. Roll a small ball of the beige fondant and flatten to make the muzzle. Attach to the face with water. Use the ball tool to create eye sockets.

24 Mix a little grain alcohol to the edible pink dust and paint on the inside of the mouth. To make the ears, press two pea-sized balls of the dark brown fondant into flat circles, and then pinch the base together to cup them. Attach them to the head using a little water.

Use scissors to create the hands.

Taper the arms so that they are narrower and flatter at the upper end.

Score lines using the wheel tool.

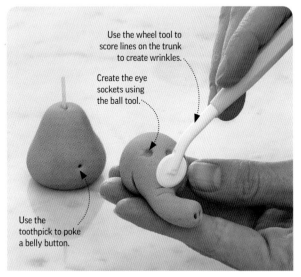

Use the wheel tool to score lines on the trunk to create wrinkles.

Create the eye sockets using the ball tool.

Use the toothpick to poke a belly button.

25 Roll four small sausages of dark brown fondant for the arms and legs. Flatten the legs at the ends and dry for 1 hour. Cut four circles of the beige fondant and attach inside the ears and at the bottom of the legs with water. Attach the limbs to the body with royal icing and let dry overnight.

26 For the elephant, roll a ball of pale-gray fondant into a pear shape and insert a piece of dry spaghetti into it. Roll another ball of the same size, molding some of the fondant into a sausage on one side to create a trunk. Poke two holes in the trunk with the end of a paintbrush.

In the Jungle 93

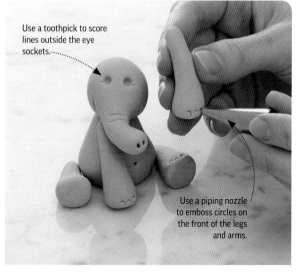

Use a toothpick to score lines outside the eye sockets.

Use a piping nozzle to emboss circles on the front of the legs and arms.

Place two tiny balls of black fondant into the sockets.

Place two tiny dots of white fondant on the eyes to create a glint.

Squash the ears slightly to give an oval, curved appearance.

27 Roll out two sausages to create the arms, tapering at the top, and flatten the bottom. Attach with some royal icing. Repeat for the legs and affix to the sides of the torso. Roll out two thick circles of gray fondant for the ears and use the ball tool to create a shallow cavity in the center of each.

28 Emboss a mouth using the back of a small knife. Roll out a little flesh-colored fondant thinly and cut out circles to fit the cavity in the ears. Moisten the back with water and press into place. Spread a little royal icing on the edge of each ear and affix to the head. Let dry overnight.

29 Using the craft glue, attach the green satin ribbon around the base of the cake drum to give a neat finish. Place the lion on the cake. Place the snake on the top of the cake, in between the treetops.

30 Finally, place the elephant and the monkey on the cake drum and insert the giraffe into the center of the cake.

Animal Cupcakes

Create some lovely jungle-inspired cupcakes by piping green-tinted buttercream frosting through a "grass" piping nozzle. Circles of leftover fondant can be used to make tiger, hippo, and giraffe faces. Roll the fondant very thinly, and use circular cutters in a variety of sizes to produce eyes, muzzles, and ears. Mix a little brown coloring paste with grain alcohol to paint on whiskers and spots, and assemble using a little water, before placing on the piped cupcakes.

Use a wide-tipped brush to stipple markings on the animals.

You can use bright fondants to create different animal faces.

Soccer Mania

This is a remarkably simple cake to make, and the scarf can be adjusted to match the colors of your child's favorite team. With its bright green fondant-covered cake drum and strands of fondant grass dotted around the sides, it is the ideal cake for soccer fans of any age.

PREP 1 hr **BAKE** 35-45 mins **DECORATE** 2 hrs, plus overnight drying time **SERVES** 10-15

Ingredients

- cornstarch, for dusting
- 1lb 2oz (500g) green fondant, strengthened (see p176)
- 8in (20cm) hemisphere cake (baked in a specialty pan or an ovenproof bowl), cut in half horizontally, sandwiched with buttercream, and crumb coated (see p171)
- ²⁄₃ cup (7oz/200g) buttercream frosting (see p180)
- confectioner's sugar, for dusting
- 9oz (250g) white fondant
- 5½oz (150g) black fondant
- 1lb 2oz (500g) red fondant
- 10oz (300g) blue fondant

Equipment

- fondant roller
- 12in (30cm) round cake drum
- fondant smoother
- sharp knife
- palette knife
- large hexagon cutter (see p187 for template)
- large pentagon cutter (see p187 for template)
- pizza cutter (optional)
- 3¼ft (1m) blue satin ribbon, ½in (1cm) wide
- craft glue

1 Dust a surface with cornstarch and roll out the strengthened green fondant to about ¹⁄₈in (3mm) thick. It should be large enough to cover the entire cake drum. Brush the drum with a little water and cover with the fondant, using the smoother to create an even surface. Cut off the excess using a sharp knife. Let dry overnight. Wrap the remaining green fondant in plastic wrap for later use.

2 Place the crumb-coated cake on a sheet of parchment paper. Lightly cover the surface with a thin layer of buttercream frosting, using the palette knife to make it as smooth as possible.

3 Dust a surface with confectioner's sugar, roll out the white fondant to ⅛in (3mm) thick, and cut out 10–15 hexagons, using the hexagon cutter (see p187 for template). Cover the excess fondant in plastic wrap and set aside for later use.

4 On the dusted surface, roll out the black fondant to about ⅛in (3mm) thick and cut out 5–10 pentagons, using the pentagon cutter (see p187 for template). Wrap the excess black fondant in plastic wrap and set aside for later use.

Position the black pentagon carefully in the center.

5 Brush the back of a black pentagon with a little water and place it on the top of the cake. Brush the backs of the white hexagons with water, one at a time, and carefully press them into place around the pentagon, so that the edges are flush where they meet and the surface is smooth.

6 Roll out more hexagons and pentagons, if needed, and add them to the surface of the ball to create the classic soccer-ball pattern. Build up the shapes to cover the whole surface. When you reach the base, cut off any excess and smooth with the fondant smoother. Let set overnight.

7 When the cake has set, move it to the center of the covered drum using a palette knife.

8 Dust a surface with confectioner's sugar and roll out the red fondant (or a fondant to match your child's team colors) to about ¹/₈in (3mm) thick. Use a pizza cutter or a sharp knife to cut a rectangular strip, about 14in x 2¹/₂in (36cm x 6cm).

Roll out the fondant on a surface dusted with confectioner's sugar.

9 Brush water all around the lower side of the cake, to the height of about 2¹/₂in (6cm) up from the drum. Carefully wrap the red fondant strip around the cake so that it meets at the front. Fold the extra length back on itself and attach with a little water.

10 Roll out some of the blue fondant to ¹/₈in (3mm) thick. Using a pizza cutter, cut a rectangular strip, 14in x 2¹/₂in (36cm x 6cm). Cut this further into 7–8 rectangles, 1¹/₂in (4cm) wide.

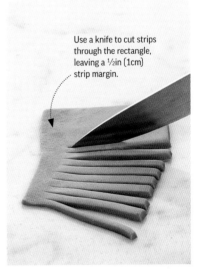

Use a knife to cut strips through the rectangle, leaving a ½in (1cm) strip margin.

11 Brush the backs of the blue strips with a little water and place them, one by one, on the red fondant scarf at regular intervals.

12 While the fondant is soft, use a sharp knife to score little sideways Vs into the surface of the scarf to create the appearance of knitting stitches. Continue until the whole scarf is scored.

13 Dust a surface with confectioner's sugar and roll out the remaining blue fondant to about ⅛in (3mm) thick. Cut a rectangle, about 2½in x 2in (6cm x 5cm) to create the end of the scarf.

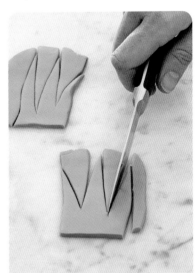

14 Score the end of the blue fondant strip with Vs, brush the back with a little water, and carefully affix to the end of the folded-over red scarf.

15 Dust a surface with confectioner's sugar, roll out the remaining green fondant to ⅛in (3mm) thick, and cut out tufts of grass with a knife.

16 Brush the backs of the tufts with water and attach around the base of the scarf in an uneven pattern.

17 Affix the blue ribbon around the base of the cake drum with a little craft glue.

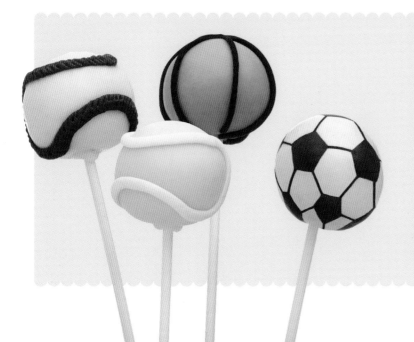

Cake-pop Sports Balls

Create these fabulous sporty cake pops (see pp172–3) to accompany your cake. For the baseball cake pop, dip the pop in melted white candy melts and pipe on red royal icing, using a small star tip. For the tennis ball, dip the cake pop in pale yellow candy melts and pipe white royal icing. For the basketball, cover in orange candy melts and pipe black royal icing from top to base around the pop, to form seams. For the soccer ball, dip the pop in white candy melts, let dry, and mark the pattern using an edible black pen.

Animal cupcakes

Create a menagerie of animal cupcakes using these quirky and creative decoration ideas. You can use your child's favorite candies to re-create their favorite animal in cupcake form.

White chocolate chips

White mini marshmallows

Brown fondant

Black writing icing

Fluffy sheep

Chocolate matchsticks

Chocolate chips

Large and small candy-coated chocolate candies

Chocolate hedgehog

Yellow candy-coated chocolate candies

Chocolate sprinkles

Black licorice

Triangle chocolate bar segment

Pink jelly bean

Red and black licorice ropes

Bright-eyed cat

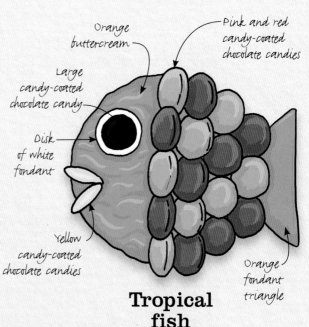

Orange buttercream

Large candy-coated chocolate candy

Disk of white fondant

Pink and red candy-coated chocolate candies

Yellow candy-coated chocolate candies

Orange fondant triangle

Tropical fish

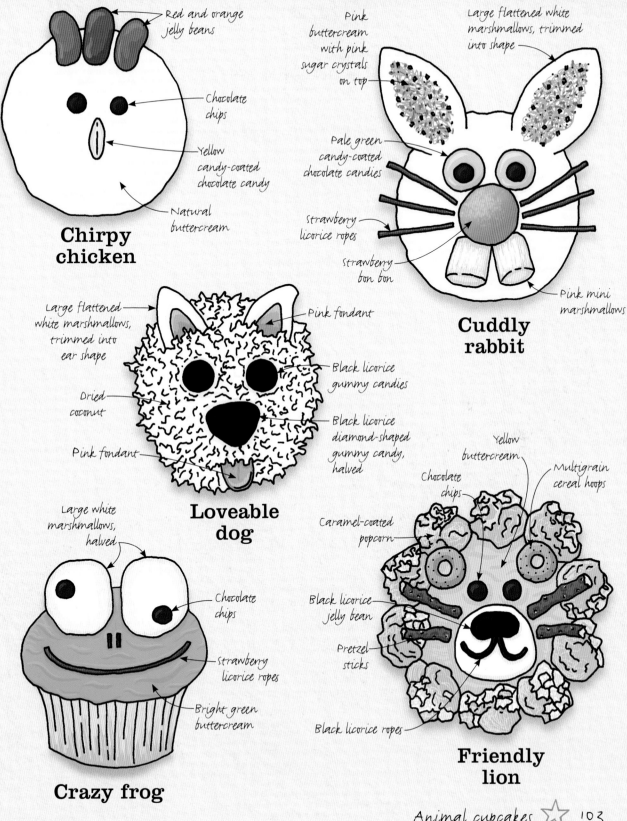

Chirpy chicken

Red and orange jelly beans

Chocolate chips

Yellow candy-coated chocolate candy

Natural buttercream

Cuddly rabbit

Pink buttercream with pink sugar crystals on top

Large flattened white marshmallows, trimmed into shape

Pale green candy-coated chocolate candies

strawberry licorice ropes

strawberry bon bon

Pink mini marshmallows

Loveable dog

Large flattened white marshmallows, trimmed into ear shape

Pink fondant

Black licorice gummy candies

Dried coconut

Black licorice diamond-shaped gummy candy, halved

Pink fondant

Crazy frog

Large white marshmallows, halved

Chocolate chips

Strawberry licorice ropes

Bright green buttercream

Friendly lion

Yellow buttercream

Multigrain cereal hoops

Chocolate chips

Caramel-coated popcorn

Black licorice jelly bean

Pretzel sticks

Black licorice ropes

Prima Ballerina

This lovely ballet cake is lightly frosted with buttercream, wrapped in white fondant, and adorned with satin ribbons held in place with royal icing. The beautiful ballerina is hand-modeled and held in position with spaghetti. Piping buttercream ruffles on the board means you won't need to cover it.

 PREP 50–60 mins   **BAKE** 25–30 mins   **DECORATE** 3¾ hrs, plus overnight drying time   **SERVES** 20

Ingredients

- 2 x 8in (20cm) round vanilla sponge cakes (see p164)
- ⅔ cup (7oz/200g) vanilla buttercream frosting
- confectioner's sugar, for dusting
- 2lb 2oz (1kg) white fondant
- 1½ cups (1lb 2oz/500g) pale pink buttercream frosting

For the ballerina
- 1¾oz (50g) flesh fondant, strengthened
- edible black pen
- edible pink dust
- 1oz (25g) brown fondant, strengthened
- dry spaghetti
- 1oz (25g) white fondant, strengthened
- grain alcohol
- ⅓ cup royal icing
- 1¾oz (50g) pink fondant, strengthened

Equipment

- 10in (25cm) round cake drum
- fondant roller
- 2 fondant smoothers
- sharp knife
- small artist's paintbrush
- 20in x ⅛in (50cm x 3mm) pink satin ribbon

continued on the next page...

1 Sandwich and crumb coat the cakes with vanilla buttercream frosting (see pp170–1). Place them in the fridge and allow to firm for 30 minutes. Remove from the fridge and carefully place on the center of a cake drum, using a dollop of buttercream frosting on the cake drum to keep the cake in place. Lightly frost with another layer of buttercream.

2 Dust a surface with confectioner's sugar, and roll out the white fondant to about ¼in (5mm) thick in a circle large enough to cover the cake. Carefully lift the fondant over the top of the cake and smooth down the sides using a fondant smoother (see pp178–9). Trim the excess fondant with a sharp knife and leave to set overnight.

- 30 x 3in (80 x 7cm) fine pink net
- needle and pink thread
- round piping tip (Wilton no. 1)
- petal piping tip (Wilton no. 150)
- piping bag
- 3¼ft (1m) pink satin ribbon, 1¼in (3cm) wide
- 9¾ft (3m) pink satin ribbon, ¾in (2cm) wide
- craft glue

Ballerina hair

Alternatively, press brown fondant through a clean garlic press to create strands of hair. Attach them to the head with water while they are still moist.

3 Use two smoothers—one on the top and one on the side—to get a crisp edge at the top. Smooth in a downward motion to ensure that any trapped air bubbles are released at the base of the cake. Press the two smoothers together at the edges of the cake to get a neat line.

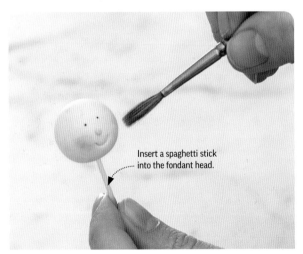

Insert a spaghetti stick into the fondant head.

4 To make the ballerina, form a cherry-sized ball from the flesh-colored fondant for the head. Make a tiny nose from the fondant and place on the face. Emboss a mouth with the tip of a piping nozzle and mark two eyes using the edible black pen. Brush the cheeks with the edible pink dust and set aside.

5 Roll strengthened brown fondant to create strands of hair, and attach with a little water to the ballerina's head around the face. Roll a few strands of fondant into a bun and attach to the back of the head.

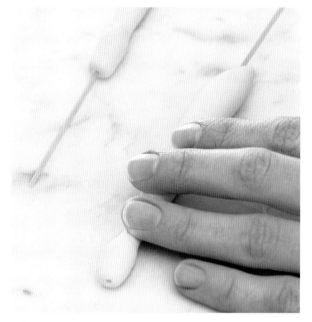

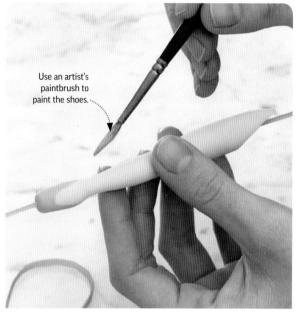

6 Take two lengths of spaghetti and model two slender legs around them using a small amount of white fondant, with feet *en pointe* (on the tips of the toes). Ensure that about 2in (5cm) spaghetti extends from both ends, to insert into the cake.

Use an artist's paintbrush to paint the shoes.

7 Mix together some pink dust with the grain alcohol and paint on the ballet shoes. Use the ⅛in (3mm) pink ribbon for the laces criss-crossing halfway up the calves, attaching them with royal icing. Set aside to dry, ideally overnight.

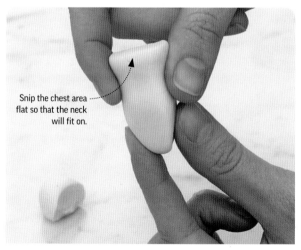

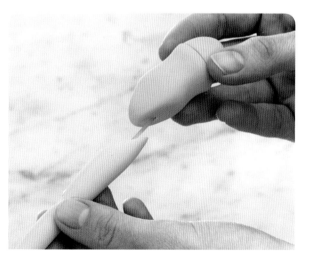

Snip the chest area flat so that the neck will fit on.

8 Use a walnut-sized ball of strengthened pink fondant to create a slender torso and hips. Form the neck and upper torso using a small amount of the flesh-colored fondant. Use a strand of dry spaghetti to poke a hole where the legs will fit later. Let dry, ideally overnight.

9 Once the torso is dry, carefully attach the legs by slipping the lengths of spaghetti into the torso. Moisten the top of the legs to make sure they stick.

10 Form two elegant arms from a small ball of the flesh-colored fondant, using fine scissors to create fingers. Shape the arms so that they can be attached to the torso upright, in a classic *en haut* (over the head) position. Let dry, ideally overnight.

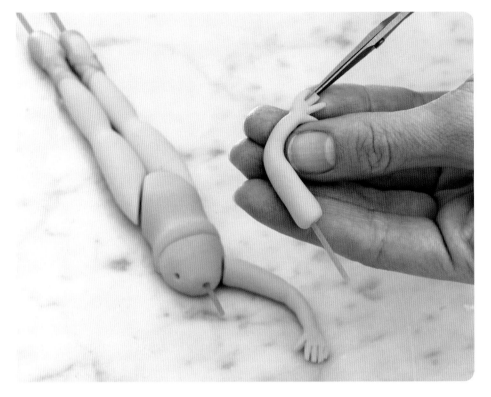

11 Fold the pink net in half lengthwise, then gather it into an accordian shape. String the netting together using a needle and thread to create a tutu. Leave enough thread at both ends to tie the tutu to the ballerina once she is dry. The tutu should be just wide enough to fit around the waist of the ballerina.

12 Roll a long, thin rope of pink fondant and cut into six short lengths. Attach one around the bun and two as shoulder straps. Flatten one slightly to form a band around the top of the bodice. Roll the remaining two into tiny roses, one for the bodice and one for the bun, and attach with a little water.

13 Once the ballerina is dry and all of the elements are secure, lay the ballerina on her front and place the tutu around her waist. Use the thread to draw the ends of the tutu together, and trim any excess netting. Tie the tutu in place, around her waist, using the excess threads, snipping stray threads with sharp scissors.

14 Attach the round piping tip to a piping bag and fill with royal icing. Cut two lengths of the ³/₄in (2cm) wide ribbon, each long enough to wrap once around the cake. Pipe tiny dots of royal icing to glue the ribbon to the cake. Affix one ribbon at the base of the cake and one at the top, wrapping them in a criss-cross pattern and bringing together at the front. Create a large bow with the 1¹/₄in (3cm) wide ribbon, and use royal icing to attach it just above where the bands meet.

15 Attach the petal tip to a piping bag and fill with the buttercream frosting. Working your way around the cake board, from the outer edge of the board inward, pipe three rows of ruffles, one row at a time, to create the impression of a frilled skirt. Cover all available space on the board.

The fondant should be firm to the touch.

Ruffles

To achieve even ruffles, squeeze out a length of buttercream and fold it back over itself. Apply firm pressure as you pipe the buttercream around the cake.

Ruffles should be piped close together.

Ballet Shoe Cupcakes

Spread a little buttercream frosting on the top of the cupcakes, and cover with a disk of white fondant, rolled to about ¼in (5mm) thick. Set aside. Use a fondant smoother to give them a polished finish.

Use strengthened pink fondant to hand-model tiny ballet shoes (one per cupcake), using the small end of the ball tool to create a cavity. Use sharp scissors to cut ribbons about 2in (5cm) long. Create slots for the ribbons on the sides of each shoe with a knife, and press the end of a length of ribbon into each. Use a knife to emboss a line around the opening of the shoes. Affix to the top of the cupcakes with a little royal icing, and let dry for 1 hour before displaying.

Press in the end of a small piping tip to create the loops of a bow.

Score in the ribbons using a sharp knife.

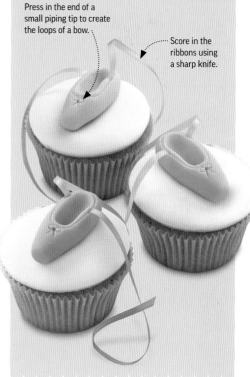

16 Loop the ¾in (1.5cm) wide ribbon around the base of the drum, and attach with a little craft glue. Set aside to dry. Carefully attach the ballerina to the top of the cake, pushing the spaghetti into the surface to provide support—a dot of royal icing under her feet will help to keep her in place.

Fish Tank Friends

Capture the seaside in a fish tank, with this simple, buttercream-covered sponge cake, cut to shape, frosted, and decorated with sugar-coated licorice and colorful fondant fish and sea creatures. Gorgeous crab and starfish cupcakes on the side complete this aquatic theme.

 PREP 1 hr   **BAKE** 35–45 mins   **DECORATE** 3–4 hrs, plus overnight drying time   **SERVES** 25

Ingredients

- cornstarch, for dusting
- 14oz (400g) pale-blue fondant, strengthened (see p176)
- 3½oz (100g) orange fondant, strengthened
- 1oz (25g) white fondant, strengthened
- 1oz (25g) black fondant, strengthened
- 1¾oz (50g) each red, lilac, and aqua fondant, strengthened
- 1oz (25g) yellow fondant, strengthened
- 2 x 8in (20cm) square sponge cakes (see p164), cut in half, sandwiched with buttercream and crumb coated (see p171)
- 2 cups (1lb 4oz/600g) buttercream frosting (see p180)
- aqua food coloring paste
- brown food coloring paste
- edible gold glitter, or ¼ cup light brown sugar
- sugar-coated licorice ropes, green and red

Equipment

- fondant roller and smoother
- 12in x 8in (30cm x 20cm) rectangular cake drum

continued on the next page...

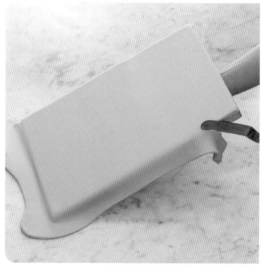

1 Dust a surface with cornstarch and roll out the pale-blue fondant to about ⅛in (3mm) thick. It should be large enough to cover the cake drum. Moisten the drum with a little water and cover with the fondant, using the fondant smoother to achieve a perfect finish (see p179). Trim off the excess, cover with plastic wrap, and set aside for later use. Let the cake drum dry overnight.

2 To make the fish, roll orange fondant into a cherry-sized ball and flatten with your hands to make the body. Roll a small ball of white fondant, flatten slightly, top with a tiny dot of black fondant, and place on the head to make the eyes. Roll another ball of orange fondant and model into a tail. Make different kinds of fish in varying sizes using red and lilac fondants. Make a larger goldfish tail for the top of the cake. Let everything dry overnight.

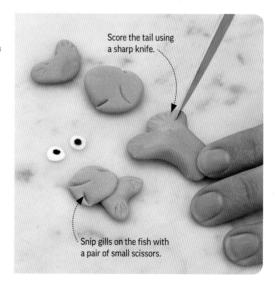

Score the tail using a sharp knife.

Snip gills on the fish with a pair of small scissors.

- sharp knife
- small scissors
- star cutter
- round piping tip (Wilton no. 2)
- palette knife
- 3¼ft (1m) blue satin ribbon, ½in (1cm) wide
- craft glue

Marbling

Mix a little red fondant with a tiny ball of white fondant and blend to get a marbled effect. Use the two-toned fondant to create fish, as shown in step 2.

3 To make the seaweed, dust a surface with cornstarch, roll out the aqua fondant to about ¹⁄₁₆in (2mm) thick, and cut thin ribbons. Holding the ends of one ribbon at a time, twist, and let dry for 1 day.

Create curved upward tips with your fingers.

Gently emboss the surface using the end of a piping tip.

4 For the starfish, dust a surface with cornstarch and roll out the remaining lilac fondant to about ¹⁄₁₆–¹⁄₈in (2–3mm) thick. Using the star cutter, cut out several star shapes. Repeat with the yellow fondant, and let the starfish dry for 1 day.

Keep the top and side edges crisp and sharp.

Swirl the buttercream frosting using a palette knife to create a watery effect.

5 Place the cake on a sheet of parchment paper. Put three-quarters of the buttercream frosting into a separate bowl. Add 1 teaspoon of the aqua coloring paste and mix well. Cover the cake with the aqua buttercream frosting using a palette knife. To smooth the edges, dip the palette knife in warm water and run it over the buttercream frosting.

6 Add ¼ teaspoon of the brown food coloring paste to the remaining untinted buttercream frosting and mix well. Using a palette knife, paddle the brown frosting around the bottom of the cake, so that it is textured and slightly rippled.

7 While the buttercream frosting is still soft, press the gold glitter onto the brown frosting to create the look of sand (you can also use light brown sugar for this). Put the cake aside to set for 2–3 hours.

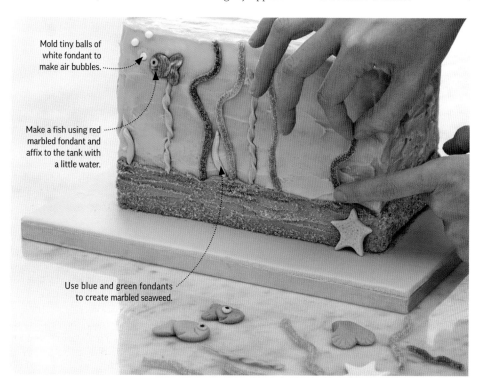

Mold tiny balls of white fondant to make air bubbles.

Make a fish using red marbled fondant and affix to the tank with a little water.

Use blue and green fondants to create marbled seaweed.

8 Carefully move the cake to the covered cake drum. Attach all the sea elements to the cake using a little water. Cut the licorice ropes and press into the buttercream frosting in wavy patterns. Snip off any excess at the top. Press the goldfish tail onto the top of the cake. Finally, affix the blue ribbon in place around the base of the covered drum, using craft glue.

Under the Sea Cupcakes

Use a large round tip to pipe yellow buttercream frosting onto the surface of the cupcakes, top with glitter, and then create sea creatures to decorate. A smiling starfish can be modeled using lilac fondant. Model a crab from deep pink fondant, creating eyes on stalks. For the coral, roll tiny balls of orange fondant and create a cavity with the end of a paintbrush. Score the surface of short ropes of green fondant for seaweed. All creatures need to harden for a few hours before you affix them to the cupcakes, using a little water.

Sea creatures

If you've got some spare time, why not try making some fishy cake pops (see p73) in a range of colors or use some leftover fondant to make some cheeky octopuses (see p72).

Press spaghetti sticks into a ball of white fondant and smooth down for the eyes.

Score a mouth with a circular cutter.

Use scissors to snip a small V-shape for the claws.

Try using yellow sugar crystals instead of glitter.

Score with the end of a fine piping tip, or a star cutter.

Hand-modeling the lilac fondant gives a more realistic shape than using a cutter.

Blue paper cupcake liners complete the underwater theme.

Take one *cake pop...*

One cake pop—12 different ideas to wow your party guests! Get creative and mold your cake pop into some weird and wonderful shapes then decorate with brightly-colored candy melts.

Pink fondant

Green fondant

Edible pen

Red candy melts

Apple

Molded white fondant

Red sugar sprinkles

Blue candy melts

Brown candy melts

Edible pen

Band of white fondant

Piece of cake

Turquoise candy melts

Gold luster dust

Pink rice paper sprinkles

White fondant

Edible pen

Little star

Ivory candy melts

Edible pen

Green fondant disk

Edible pen

Eyeball

Cover pop in white melts

Edible pen

Sheet of white fondant

Ghost

Red candy-coated chocolate candy

Rice paper sprinkles

Purple/pink candy melts

Brown candy melts

Ivory candy melts

Cupcakes

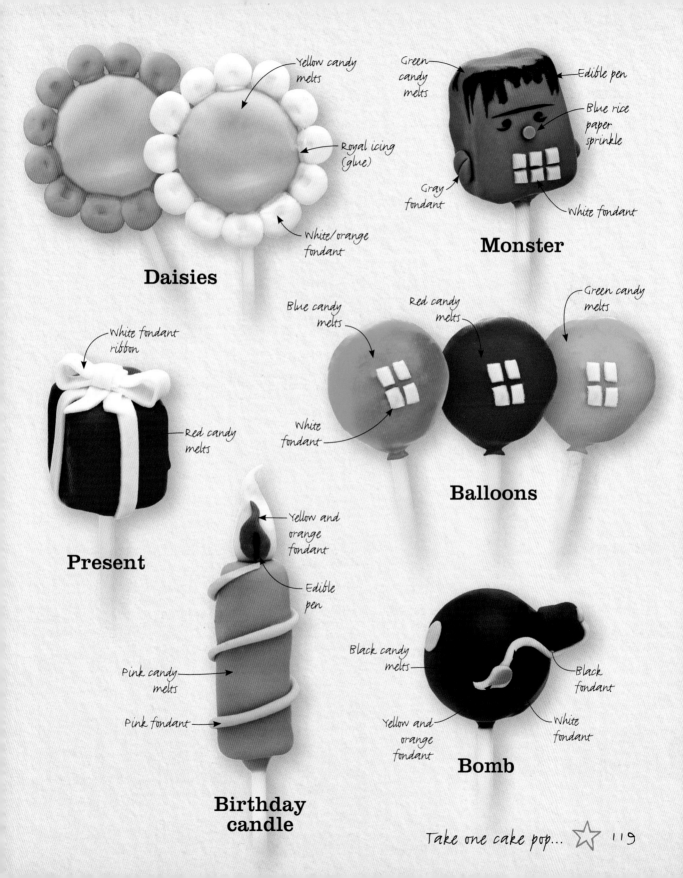

Yellow candy melts

Royal icing (glue)

White/orange fondant

Daisies

Green candy melts

Edible pen

Blue rice paper sprinkle

Gray fondant

White fondant

Monster

White fondant ribbon

Red candy melts

Present

Blue candy melts

Red candy melts

Green candy melts

White fondant

Balloons

Yellow and orange fondant

Edible pen

Pink candy melts

Pink fondant

Birthday candle

Black candy melts

Black fondant

Yellow and orange fondant

White fondant

Bomb

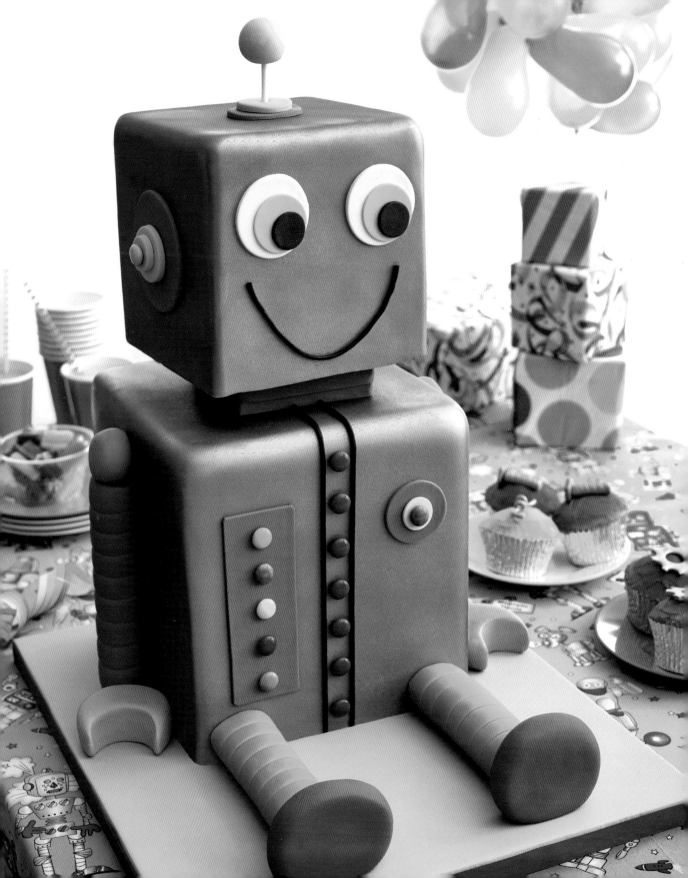

Happy Robot

This cheerful robot is surprisingly easy to make, although care must be taken to support its large head with dowels and smaller cake boards. Spray with silver luster, decorate with candies of your choice, top with a cake-pop antenna, and prepare to delight a crowd.

 PREP 1–1½ hrs   **BAKE** 1–1½ hrs   **DECORATE** 4 hrs, plus overnight drying time   **SERVES** 30-40

Ingredients

- confectioner's sugar, for dusting
- 2lb (900g) pale-green fondant, strengthened (see p176)
- 4 x 8in (20cm) square cakes (see p186), layers sandwiched with buttercream to reach 8in (20cm) high and crumb coated (see p171)
- 3 x 6in (15cm) square cakes (see p186), layers sandwiched with buttercream to reach 6in (15cm) high and crumb coated (see p171)
- 9lb (4kg) pale-gray fondant
- 3 x 100ml can silver luster spray
- ¼ cup royal icing (see p181)
- 14oz (400g) red fondant, strengthened
- 14oz (400g) bright-blue fondant, strengthened
- 1¾oz (50g) deep-yellow fondant, strengthened
- 1oz (25g) each pale-blue, white, purple, and lemon-yellow fondant
- 1oz (25g) black fondant
- black licorice ropes
- candy-coated chocolate buttons
- 1 cake pop, on stick, dipped in yellow candy melts (see pp172–3)

continued on the next page...

1 Dust a surface with confectioner's sugar and roll out the strengthened green fondant to about ⅛in (3mm) thick, so that it is large enough to cover the surface of the larger cake drum. Moisten the surface of the drum. Cover the drum with the fondant, using the fondant smoother to create a smooth surface. Let dry overnight.

2 Place the larger cake on the 8in (20cm) board. Dust a surface with confectioner's sugar and roll out the some of the pale-gray fondant to about ¼in (5mm) thick. Carefully cover the larger cake and board with the fondant and use the fondant smoother for an even surface. Trim off the excess fondant around the base using a sharp knife. Place the smaller cake on the 6in (15cm) board, roll out the gray fondant again, and cover as above. Wrap the excess under the cake so that the bottom is almost covered. Let dry overnight.

Equipment

- fondant roller
- 16 x 14in (40 x 35cm) rectangular cake drum
- fondant smoother
- 8in (20cm) square cake board
- sharp knife
- 6in (15cm) square cake board
- 2 x 4in (10cm) square cake drums
- 4 plastic dowels, at least 8in (20cm) in height
- wire cutters or pruning shears
- craft glue
- 6½ft (2m) red satin ribbon, ½in (1cm) wide
- blade tool
- 5 circular cutters— 3in (7.5cm), 2¼in (6cm), 2in (5cm), 1½in (4cm), ¾in (2cm)
- piping bag
- small round piping tip (Wilton no. 4)

3 When the fondant has set and become slightly harder and firmer to the touch, spray both the cakes with silver luster spray, holding the can about 8in (20cm) away from the surface of the cake to provide an even finish. You may wish to spray the cakes on a newspaper-covered surface, since the spraying process can be messy. Let dry and then carefully move the cake to the covered cake drum.

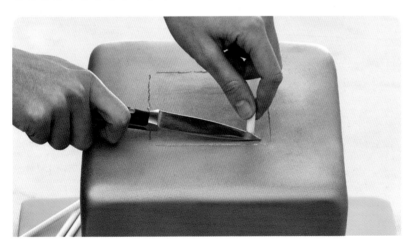

4 Place one of the 4in (10cm) cake drums on the top of the larger cake and center carefully. Gently press into the cake to emboss the surface, and then remove. Insert a dowel just inside the embossed mark and score it with a sharp knife at the point that it touches the top of the cake. Remove and cut the dowel at this mark using wire cutters. Cut the three remaining dowels to the same length.

5 Glue the two 4in (10cm) drums together to give extra height and affix two lengths of red ribbon all around the edges, using craft glue.

 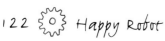

6 Insert a dowel into each of the four corners of the embossed square. Dab a little royal icing on the dowels and carefully place the covered drum on the cake, taking care to fit it neatly over the embossed square.

Score the surface of the limbs with the blade tool.

7 For the arms and legs, roll two sausages each of the red and blue fondants. Roll and flatten two large balls of red fondant for the feet. Roll out some of the red fondant thinly, and cut a rectangle, 2in x 5in (5cm x 12cm), for the front panel.

For the hands, cut out half-moon-shapes from the deep-yellow circles.

8 Roll two golf-ball-sized balls of bright blue fondant for the upper arms and flatten slightly. Roll out the deep-yellow fondant to ³/₄in (2cm) thick and cut out two circles with the 2in (5cm) circular cutter for the hands.

9 Roll out the pale-blue fondant to ¹/₄in (5mm) thick, and cut three circles using the 1¹/₂in (4cm) cutter, two using the 2in (5cm) cutter, and two using the ³/₄in (2cm) cutter. Then, roll out the white fondant to ¹/₄in (5mm) thick, and cut out two circles, using the 2¹/₄in (6cm) circular cutter.

Roll all the fondant thinly on a dusted surface.

Layer one red and one blue circle on the head to hold the antenna later.

10 Cut out one 1¹/₂in (4cm) circle from the purple fondant. Next, cut one ³/₄in (2cm) circle out of the lemon-yellow fondant and two from the black. Cut one 2in (5cm) circle and two 3in (7.5cm) circles from the remaining red fondant.

11 Layer the white, blue, and black circles on the smaller cake, using a little water, to create the eyes. Place one red and two blue circles on each side of the head for the ears. Attach them using a little water.

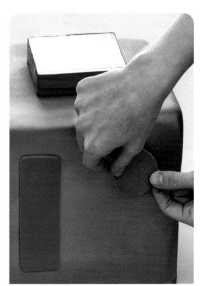

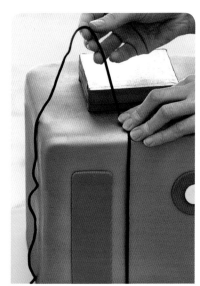

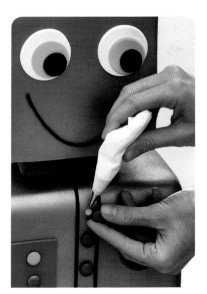

12 Affix the red rectangle to the front of the body with water. Attach the purple and lemon-yellow circles next to the rectangle with water.

13 Use licorice ropes for the front of the body and the mouth, attaching them using a little royal icing.

14 Attach the head to the top of the body using royal icing. Use more royal icing to glue rows of candies on the front of the body and the ears.

Stick the cake pop on the top of the head.

Nuts and Bolts Cupcakes

These bright "robotic" cupcakes (see pp174–5) are great for feeding extra guests or filling goody bags. Use a palette knife to frost cupcakes with buttercream colored with different food coloring pastes. Use plenty of paste to get a nice rich color.

For the spring cupcake, roll a thin rope of strengthened fondant and then wrap it in spirals around a pen and let it dry overnight. When dry, slip off the pen and cut into pieces. For the nut cupcake, cut out strengthened fondant circles using a cutter, and then cut a circle from the center of each. Use the end of a large circular piping tip to cut out semicircles from the perimeter.

For the bolt cupcake, roll a thicker rope of strengthened fondant and score the surface with a knife to create the threads. Cut into lengths. Use a hexagon cutter to cut small tops for the bolts and affix to the scored ropes with water. Let dry until just hard, and spray with silver luster, one side at a time.

15 To assemble the robot, attach the arms and legs to the body using royal icing or water. Top the arms with the blue balls, and attach the red feet to the legs. Affix the ribbon around the base, using craft glue. Just before displaying, place the orange hands in place at the base of the arms.

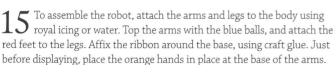

Sparkly Butterfly

Simply carve this beautiful butterfly out of a sheet cake, and decorate each wing before displaying around a buttercream-frosted body coated in sprinkles. Experiment with a range of colors and candies to bring your butterfly cake to life.

 PREP 40 mins   **BAKE** 30-45 mins   **DECORATE** 3-4 hrs, plus overnight drying time   **SERVES** 20

Ingredients

- cornstarch, for dusting
- 1lb 2oz (500g) pale-green fondant, strenghtened (see p176)
- 12in (30cm) sheet cake, 3in (7.5cm) thick (see p164 and p186)
- ¾ cup (10oz/300g) buttercream frosting, tinted pink (see p180)
- ⅔ cup (7oz/200g) buttercream frosting, tinted yellow
- ⅔ cup (7oz/200g) buttercream frosting, tinted purple
- ⅔ cup (7oz/200g) buttercream frosting, tinted turquoise
- 1¾oz (50g) edible yellow glitter
- 1¾oz (50g) edible purple glitter
- 9oz (250g) white fondant, strengthened
- 3½oz (100g) multicolored sprinkles
- assorted candies—jelly beans, white chocolate disks topped with sprinkles, sprinkles, licorice, candy-coated chocolate buttons, red licorice ropes
- edible gold spray (or paint)
- 1oz (25g) silver balls

continued on the next page...

1 Dust a surface with cornstarch and roll out the pale-green fondant to about ⅛in (3mm) thick. It should be large enough to cover the cake drum. Use a pastry brush to moisten the drum with a little water and cover the drum with the fondant, then carefully smooth the fondant (see p179). Cut off any excess with a sharp knife and let dry overnight.

2 Place the sheet cake in the freezer for about 1 hour, until just beginning to freeze. Trace the template (see p187) onto a sheet of parchment paper, and cut out the individual elements. Press them down onto the surface of the slightly frozen cake, and cut around each with a serrated knife. Crumb coat each of the elements (see p171) with a little buttercream frosting and refrigerate for 30–60 minutes, or until set.

Equipment

- fondant roller
- 12in (30cm) square cake drum
- pastry brush
- fondant smoother
- serrated knife
- palette knife
- side scraper (optional)
- 1 cake-pop stick, cut in half
- 3¼ft (1m) pink satin ribbon, ½in (1cm) wide
- craft glue

3 Set the cakes for the two top parts of the wings on a large piece of parchment paper. Using the palette knife, apply the pink buttercream frosting. Reserve the remaining frosting for later use. You can also use a side scraper, to achieve a smooth surface.

4 Repeat for the other parts of the wings, frosting two in yellow frosting, two in purple frosting, and two in turquoise frosting. While still soft, press the yellow glitter onto the top of the yellow wings and purple glitter onto the purple wings. Refrigerate all of the wings for 30 minutes.

5 Cover the body section of the butterfly with the remaining pink buttercream frosting, then move to a plate and cover in multicolored sprinkles. Refrigerate for 30 minutes.

Use a palette knife to carefully place each wing on the drum.

6 To assemble the cake, arrange the body and wings as shown. Place the pink wings first, one on either side of the body, pressing them close to the body, followed by the yellow, purple, and turquoise wings.

Create three rows of silver balls to decorate the wings.

Cut licorice laces into six lengths and press into the wings.

Use jelly beans on cake-pop sticks to create antennae.

7 Spray, or paint, two chocolate buttons gold, let dry, and place on the turquoise wings along with silver balls. Press yellow licorice candies and candy-coated chocolate buttons on the yellow parts. Repeat with the pink licorice candies and pink buttons on the purple parts. Place a white chocolate disk on the pink buttercream frosting and decorate with licorice. Finally, attach the ribbon around the base of the drum, using craft glue.

Flower Power Cake Pops

Complete the theme with pretty flower cake pops. Dip cake pops in melted chocolate or brown candy melts (see p173) and, before the coating hardens, dip half of the pops into a bowl of green-tinted sugar to cover about two-thirds of each pop. Roll out some pink fondant to about 1/16in (2mm) thick and use a blossom plunger cutter to create tiny flowers and a daisy plunger cutter in two sizes to create layers for the larger flowers.

Form centers for the larger flowers with tiny balls of yellow fondant, scored with a toothpick to provide texture. Affix the layers and the center together with a little water and apply blossom and larger flowers to the cake pops with water or royal icing.

Green-tinted sprinkles or dried coconut is used to cover.

Melted chocolate or brown candy melts cover the cake pops.

sparkly Butterfly 129

Circus Big Top

This show-stopper cake is created from three sandwiched sponge cakes and an inverted bowl cake and covered with brightly-colored fondant detail. The curtains are pulled back to reveal hand-modeled circus animals and a clown.

 PREP 1½ hrs   **BAKE** 50-60 mins   **DECORATE** 4½-5 hrs, plus overnight drying time   **SERVES** 30

Ingredients

- cornstarch, for dusting
- 10oz (300g) green fondant, strengthened (see p176)
- 3 x 8in (20cm) round sponge cakes (see p164), halved and sandwiched with buttercream (see p171)
- 8in (20cm) bowl or hemisphere cake (see p164)
- 1½ cups (1lb 2oz/500g) buttercream frosting (see p180)
- confectioner's sugar, for dusting
- 1lb 2oz (500g) white fondant (see p176)
- 1lb 2oz (500g) red fondant
- 10oz (300g) black fondant
- 1lb 2oz (500g) blue fondant
- 2 tbsp royal icing
- 1lb 2oz (500g) yellow fondant
- edible black pen
- 7oz (200g) ocher fondant, strengthened (see p176)
- 3½oz (100g) dark brown fondant
- 1¾oz (50g) orange fondant, strengthened
- 3½oz (100g) gray fondant, strengthened
- ¾oz (20g) light brown fondant, strengthened
- 1oz (25g) white chocolate
- popcorn, for decorating

continued on the next page...

1 Dust a surface with cornstarch and roll out the green fondant to about ⅛in (3mm) thick, so that it is large enough to cover the cake drum. Brush the cake drum with a little water and cover with the fondant. Use the smoother to create an even surface and cut off any excess using a sharp knife. Let dry overnight. Wrap the remaining green fondant in plastic wrap for later use.

2 Place a sandwiched sponge cake on a sheet of parchment paper and paddle some buttercream on top using the palette knife. Carefully center the second sponge cake on top of this and apply some more buttercream over it. Repeat with the final cake and then place the inverted bowl cake on top of this. Crumb coat the entire surface of the cake with buttercream (see p171) and refrigerate for 1 hour, until set.

Equipment

- fondant roller
- 12in (30cm) cake drum
- fondant smoother
- sharp knife
- palette knife
- 1 plastic dowel
- 9in (23cm) cake board,
- Dresden tool
- quilting tool
- ruler
- 2 circular cutters– 2in (5cm) and 1in (2.5cm)
- 3 cake-pop sticks
- small star-shaped plunger cutter
- large spatula or cake lifter
- ball tool
- paintbrush
- 24-gauge white floral wire
- piping bag
- small round piping tip (Wilton no. 2)
- 3¼ft (1m) blue satin ribbon, ½in (1cm) wide
- craft glue

3 Once the cake has set, insert the dowel through the center of the cake, cutting off any extra that protrudes from the top. Apply a second coat of buttercream to the cake before beginning the decorations.

4 To make the roof, use the cake board as a template and draw a circle on a sheet of parchment paper. Cut around the circle, then fold it in half three times to create a neat wedge. Open the paper to get a circle marked with eight triangles.

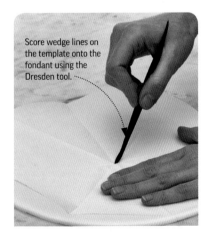

Score wedge lines on the template onto the fondant using the Dresden tool.

5 On a dusted surface, roll out the white fondant to ¹⁄₈in (3mm) thick to cover the roof template. With the template on top, cut a circle, then cut it into four wedges.

Use the quilting tool to score the surface of the wedges around the perimeter.

6 For the roof, moisten the backs of the wedges and place them opposite each other on the cake at even intervals. Cut off extra fondant to leave a cavity at the top. Trim off any excess.

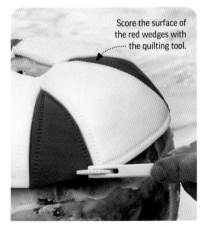

Score the surface of the red wedges with the quilting tool.

7 Repeat steps 5 and 6 using the red fondant, to get four red wedges to fit between the white wedges on the roof. Trim to size and affix with water, ensuring their edges are flush, and score.

Use the fondant smoother to get an even surface.

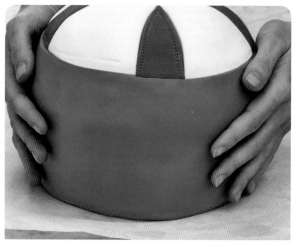

8 Dust a surface with confectioner's sugar and roll out most of the black fondant to 1/8in (3mm) thick. Use a ruler to measure the height from the base of the cake to the bottom edge of the roof. Using a sharp knife, cut out a rectangle from the fondant—as wide as the measured height, and about 6³/₄in (17.5cm) long. Moisten the back with a little water and press into position on the front of the cake. Trim off any excess.

9 Dust a surface with confectioner's sugar and roll out the blue fondant to 1/8in (3mm) thick. Using a sharp knife, cut out a rectangle that is exactly as wide as the measured height, and long enough to wrap around the cake, just covering the edges of the black rectangle on the front. Moisten the back of the rectangle and smooth into place with your hands—use the fondant smoother to achieve an even finish.

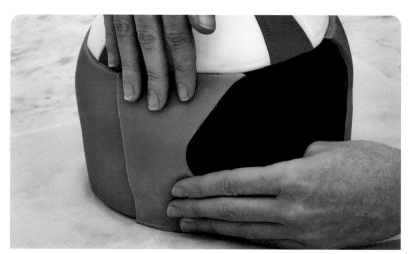

10 To make the curtains, roll out some of the remaining blue fondant again on the dusted surface to 1/8in (3mm) thick and cut out two rectangles that are exactly as tall as the height measured in step 8 and about 3in (7.5cm) wide. Cut out a curved triangle indent from one side of each curtain. Attach these on either side of the black fondant, using a little water, so that part of the curtain covers the black fondant and the remainder sits on the blue fondant wrapped around the cake.

11 To create a cap for the roof, re-roll the scraps of blue fondant on the dusted surface to 1/8in (3mm) thick. Cut out a circle using the larger circular cutter. Brush its back with water and gently press into place on the top of the roof.

12 Dust a surface with confectioner's sugar and roll out the white fondant to ¼in (5mm) thick. Using the 1in (2.5cm) circular cutter, cut out about 30 circles. Roll a thin rope of the fondant to wrap around the base of the roof.

13 Cut all the white circles in half, and attach some around the blue cap on the roof with a little water. Affix the remaining semicircles around the base of the roof on the blue fondant. Attach the white rope with water around the top of the bunting.

14 Model a cherry-sized ball of white fondant, flatten, and attach to the top of the roof with water. Roll a smaller ball for the top of the flagpole, and set aside to harden. Use a little more white fondant to model two cylindrical snack boxes. Let dry.

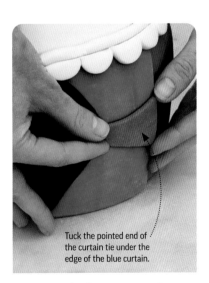

Tuck the pointed end of the curtain tie under the edge of the blue curtain.

Roll the flag over the cake-pop stick, using royal icing to secure.

15 To make the curtain ties, dust a surface with confectioner's sugar, roll out some of the red fondant to ⅛in (3mm) thick, and cut out two triangular wedges. Brush the backs with water and affix to the blue curtains.

16 To complete the popcorn snack box, roll a thin rope of the red fondant and flatten slightly. Cut the rope into tiny pieces to create stripes on the snack box.

17 For the flag, strengthen the remaining red fondant (see p176) and roll to ⅛in (3mm) thick. Cut out a rectangular piece and then cut a triangle from one end. Attach a cake-pop stick at the straight end and let dry.

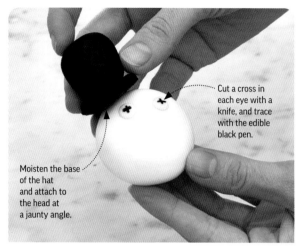

Attach the stars to the sides and the blue cap on the roof.

Cut a cross in each eye with a knife, and trace with the edible black pen.

Moisten the base of the hat and attach to the head at a jaunty angle.

18 Dust a surface with confectioner's sugar and roll out the yellow fondant to ⅛in (3mm) thick. Using the plunger cutter, cut stars to decorate the cake. Affix with a little water. Let dry. When the cake is firm, use a large spatula or cake lifter to move it to the center of the cake drum. Let dry overnight.

19 For the clown, strengthen the remaining white fondant (see p176) and roll a golf-ball-sized ball. Roll two tiny balls for the eyes and flatten. Score and attach to the face with water. For the hat, strengthen the black fondant and roll it out on a dusted surface to ⅛in (3mm) thick. Cut out a circle 1in (2.5cm) wide. Model a cylinder from the remaining fondant and attach to the circle using water. Attach the hat to the head.

Use the tip of the ball tool to create a cavity in the center of the ears.

20 To finish the clown, roll about 20 tiny balls of varying sizes from the red fondant. Attach one ball to the face with a little water to create the nose, and the others around the hat for hair. Roll a small sausage for the mouth, and attach it to the face. Score a smile using a knife. Let the clown dry, ideally for 1–2 days.

21 For the lion, model the ocher fondant into a golf-ball-sized ball for the head. Roll a smaller ball for the muzzle, flatten slightly, and attach to the face using water. Model two tiny balls for the ears and attach to the head with water. Roll a tiny ball of strengthened dark brown fondant, shape into an oval, flatten, and attach to the muzzle with water for the nose.

Use the Dresden tool to score the muzzle and the whiskers.

Use the Dresden tool to score wrinkles on the trunk.

22 For the eyes, roll two small balls of white fondant, flatten slightly with your fingers, and attach to the face using a little water. Roll two tiny balls of black fondant, flatten, and press into the white eyes. To make the mane, roll 12 pea-sized balls of the strengthened orange fondant, flatten slightly, and affix these around the head using a little water. Let dry, ideally for 1–2 days.

23 For the elephant, roll the gray fondant into a golf-ball-sized ball for the head. Roll a rope of gray fondant for the trunk and cut each end to create a flat surface.

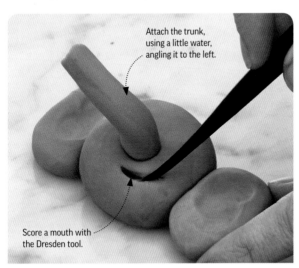

Attach the trunk, using a little water, angling it to the left.

Score a mouth with the Dresden tool.

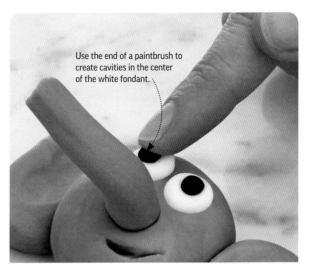

Use the end of a paintbrush to create cavities in the center of the white fondant.

24 Attach the trunk to the head using a little water, bending it slightly to the side. Roll two 1in (2.5cm) balls of the gray fondant and flatten into ovals for the ears. Use the ball tool to create indentations in the ears, smoothing all the edges as you go. Moisten the sides and press the ears onto the head, and hold in place until firm.

25 For the eyes, roll two pea-sized balls of white fondant, flatten slightly, and attach to the face, just above the trunk, using a little water. Roll two tiny balls of the black fondant and press them into the center of the white fondant eyes. Let the elephant dry, ideally for 1–2 days.

Use the tip of the ball tool to create a cavity in the center of each ear.

Mix together a little red and white fondant to create pink fondant for the nose.

Use the Dresden tool to score the muzzle.

26 To make the bear, roll a golf-ball-sized ball of the dark-brown fondant. Model a smaller ball for the muzzle, flatten slightly with your fingers, and attach to the face with water. Model two tiny balls for the ears. Moisten one side of each ear with water and press into place on the head.

27 For the eyes, roll two small balls of the white fondant, flatten slightly with your fingers, and attach to the face using a little water. Roll two tiny balls of the black fondant and press into the white eyes. Attach a tiny ball of strengthened pink fondant on the muzzle for the nose.

Score the bow with a knife to create folds.

Curl three lengths of white floral wire and press into the end of each balloon.

Use the Dresden tool to score the surface of the peanuts.

28 Make two teardrop shapes out of the red fondant for the bow. Roll a pea-sized ball for the center, and affix the bow together with water. Attach at the base of the head with water. Let dry, ideally for 1–2 days.

29 Strengthen the remaining green, blue, and yellow fondants and model into balloon shapes. Attach a small flattened ball of fondant in each color to the end of each balloon. Attach the floral wires and let dry, for 1–2 days.

30 To complete the peanut snack box, roll a very thin rope of the blue fondant and flatten slightly. Cut the rope into tiny pieces to create stripes on the box. Create peanuts using the light brown fondant. Let dry.

31 When everything is dry and hard, melt the white chocolate. Cut the cake-pop sticks in half and dip each end in the chocolate. Press one end of a cake-pop stick into the clown's head and the other end into the cake, holding the clown in place with your fingers until the chocolate hardens.

32 Attach the animals with cake-pop sticks and chocolate, until they are firmly in place on the cake. Attach the balloons to the roof with white chocolate, holding in place until firm.

Pipe scallops on the front of the flag using royal icing.

Break the popcorn into little pieces and attach to the snack box with white chocolate.

33 Decorate the flag using royal icing and let dry. Once dry, apply white chocolate to the end of the cake-pop stick and carefully push into the ball on the top of the roof. Use white chocolate to glue the smaller white fondant ball onto the top of the flagpole.

34 Attach the snack boxes on the cake drum using a little melted chocolate. Affix the popcorn on the red snack box and some peanuts on the top of the blue snack box using chocolate. Glue the remaining peanuts onto the cake drum with melted chocolate, so that they appear to tumble from the bags, and affix one at the end of the elephant's trunk.

35 Let the decorations set for 1 hour, then attach the blue ribbon around the base of the cake drum using craft glue.

Circus Party Cake Pops

Create gorgeous circus cake pops (see p172–3) for party favors or to accessorize your table. For the clown, dip the cake pop in melted white candy melts, let harden, and decorate as shown in steps 19–20.

For the popcorn box, mold the cake pop to shape, then dip in white candy melts. Once dry, draw on stripes with a red edible pen and attach a piece of popcorn to the top with white chocolate.

The bear cake pop is created by dipping a cake pop in melted brown candy melts or chocolate, and accessorizing with fondant ears, muzzle, eyes, and a length of blue ribbon at the base.

Cake *concepts*

If you're looking for a twist on a traditional cake, take a look at these cake concepts. Here you'll find inspiration for quirky centerpieces that the children can help to create, or demolish!

Wobbly rainbow

Simply allow each thin layer of gelatin to set in a mold before pouring on the next layer in another color. Allow the gelatin to cool before pouring.

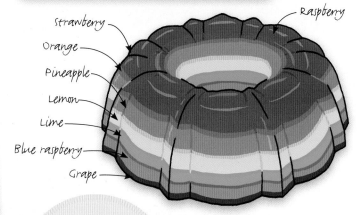

Strawberry
Orange
Pineapple
Lemon
Lime
Blue raspberry
Grape
Raspberry

Doodle on it
Frost a cake with white fondant, smooth the top and sides, and allow it to harden overnight. Supply edible pens in a variety of colors and let your child create a masterpiece!

Stack it up

Pile high a stack of delicious chocolate brownies and drizzle with melted white chocolate for the ultimate tower cake.

Ice cream sundae

Fill a cake pan with softened ice cream and broken cookies, honeycomb, or candies, then freeze until hard. Decorate with an upturned cone, a scoop of chocolate buttercream, and melted chocolate.

Easy Princess

Frost a crumb-coated bowl cake with buttercream or fondant, then affix blossoms, leaves, and vines to the surface. Carefully carve a hole from the center, and insert a plastic doll. Mold a bodice out of fondant, and attach dragées around the base and waist to draw it all together.

Use blossom cutters to cut flowers out of fondant.

Piñata

Make a chocolate piñata by painting a thick layer of melted chocolate into a bowl lined with plastic wrap. Chill until solid then turn out, remove the wrap, and affix candies on the surface using melted chocolate. Overturn on a pile of candy treasures.

Print it Have your child's favorite character printed onto a rice paper sheet. Place on top of a cake frosted with buttercream or fondant. Pipe some buttercream around the edge for an impressive finish.

Peekaboo

Cut out enough stars from pink and green sponge cakes (see p164) to run the length of your finished cake. Pour a little plain batter into a loaf pan, rest the row of stars along the length, packing them tightly so they don't move, then cover with the remaining batter and bake.

Cupcake Caterpillar

Simple, brightly colored cupcakes are linked with a star of buttercream and decorated with a variety of store-bought treats to create this jolly little caterpillar. You can add more cupcakes to feed extra guests, and with no cake to cut, the mess will be minimal.

 PREP 45 mins, plus cooling time   **BAKE** 15 mins   **DECORATE** 30–45 mins   **SERVES** 15

Ingredients

- 1½ batches of vanilla sponge cake batter, or enough to make 15 cupcakes (see p164)
- 1 tsp red food coloring paste
- 1 tsp green food coloring paste
- 1 tsp blue food coloring paste
- 1 tsp yellow food coloring paste
- 1 cup (14oz/400g) vanilla buttercream frosting (see p180)
- 2 white chocolate buttons
- ¼ cup royal icing (see p181)
- 2 blue and 1 red candy-covered chocolate drops
- 1 red liquorice rope
- 2 red jelly beans
- 14 sugar-coated gummy worms, cut in half

Equipment

- 15 plain paper cupcake liners
- 2 piping tips–small round (such as Wilton no. 2) and large open star (such as Wilton no. 2110)
- 2 piping bags: 1 large and 1 small
- palette knife
- 1 cake-pop stick, cut in half

1 Preheat the oven to 350°F (180°C). Divide the batter between four bowls, add 1 teaspoon of a single color of the food coloring paste to each bowl. Blend well to create red, blue, green, and yellow batters. Fill four cupcake liners with yellow batter, four with red, four with green, and three with blue. Bake for 15 minutes, or until the cupcakes have risen nicely and spring back to the touch. Let cool for 1 hour on a wire rack.

2 Remove the cooled cupcakes from the wire rack. On a tray or board, arrange the cupcakes on their sides in an inverted S-shape. Place the red cupcake first, followed by the green, yellow, and blue ones. End the caterpillar with the last red cupcake, reserving a green and a yellow cupcake for the head.

3 Fit the star nozzle onto the large piping bag and fill with buttercream frosting. Pipe some of the frosting onto the center of each of the cupcakes.

4 Fit the cupcakes together, in the sequence laid out in step 2, leaving the green and yellow cupcakes aside for the head of the caterpillar.

Affix the blue chocolate drops to the eyes using royal icing.

Pipe a tiny dot of royal icing onto the eyes for a glint.

5 For the face, smooth buttercream over the reserved yellow cupcake using a palette knife. Press two white-chocolate buttons onto the cupcake for the base of the eyes.

6 Use a red candy-covered chocolate drop for the nose and a liquorice rope for the mouth. Position the head onto the green cupcake, attaching it with some piped buttercream frosting.

7 Top each half of the cake-pop stick with a jelly bean and carefully poke into the caterpillar's head to form the antennae.

8 For the legs of the caterpillar, use buttercream or royal icing to attach the gummy worms to the sides of the cupcakes making up the body. Allow to set for 30 minutes before serving.

Caterpillar Cupcakes

Create these simple caterpillar faces to serve with the cake or to send out in party bags. Use plain or tinted sponge cake for the base, or add a little color by using cupcake liners in any number of colors. Simply spread with buttercream, using a palette knife, and then top with white chocolate buttons and brightly colored candy-covered chocolate drops for the eyes (with a piped dot of royal icing to create a glint). Decorate with liquorice ropes and more candies, if desired. Jelly beans on cake-pop sticks make perfect antennae.

Princess Castle

Fit for a princess, this elegant cake is created from tiered sponge cakes, iced with silky buttercream frosting, and surrounded by stacked cookie towers that have been frosted and then topped with waffle cones. A pretty princess looks down from the balcony onto a lawn full of roses.

PREP 1½ hrs   **BAKE** 50–60 mins   **DECORATE** 4½–5 hrs, plus overnight drying time   **SERVES** 30–40

Ingredients

- ⅔ cup (7oz/200g) buttercream frosting, tinted pale green (see p180)
- 2 x 8in (20cm) round sponge cakes (see p164), sandwiched with buttercream and crumb coated (see p171)
- 2 x 5½in (13cm) round sponge cakes, sandwiched with buttercream and crumb coated
- 4 cups (2lbs 3oz/1kg) ivory buttercream
- 7oz (200g) white chocolate
- 4 x 9oz (250g) package chocolate chip cookies
- 1¾oz (50g) flesh-colored fondant, strengthened (see p176)
- 1¾oz (50g) rose-colored fondant, strengthened
- dry spaghetti
- 1oz (25g) reddish-brown fondant, strengthened
- edible black pen
- 1¾oz (50g) small sugar pearls
- edible pink luster dust
- 1¾oz (50g) fuchsia fondant
- cornstarch, for dusting
- 7oz (200g) pale-pink fondant
- 1¾oz (50g) pale-green fondant
- confectioner's sugar, for dusting
- 2 small silver sugar balls

continued on the next page...

Dip the knife in warm water dry and smooth over the frosting to get an even surface.

Snip the dowels so that they are flush with the cake surface.

1 Spread some of the pale-green buttercream frosting over the cake drum using the palette knife. To achieve an even surface, dip the knife in warm water, dry, and then smooth over the frosting. Let the cake drum set overnight.

2 Place the 8in (20cm) sandwiched cakes on parchment paper. Apply the ivory buttercream frosting all over using the palette knife. Repeat with the smaller cakes. Let set overnight.

3 Move the larger cake onto the drum. Gently press the 5½in (13cm) board into the top, centering it carefully, so that it leaves an imprint. Remove, then insert the dowels into the cake.

- 4 waffle cones
- 3 tbsp royal icing (see p181)
- 1¾oz (50g) sprinkles
- 1¾oz (50g) white chocolate disk candies covered with sprinkles
- a little milk (optional)
- 3½oz (100g) white chocolate buttons
- sugar pearls
- 7oz (200g) white and pink miniature marshmallows
- 1 tsp white fondant

Equipment

- 14in (35cm) cake drum
- palette knife
- 5½in (13cm) cake board
- 4 plastic dowels
- small scissors
- small circle-tipped piping nozzle (PME no. 1)
- small artist's paintbrush
- fondant roller
- sharp knife
- toothpick
- shield-shaped cutters—3¼in (8cm) and 1½in (4cm) (see p187 for templates)
- heart-shaped cutters—1½in (4cm) and ½in (1cm)
- 1 cake-pop stick
- serrated knife
- piping bag
- 4in (10cm) thin pink satin ribbon
- 3¼ft (1m) pink satin ribbon, ½in (1cm) wide
- craft glue

4 Place the smaller cake on the 5½in (13cm) cake board, holding it in place with buttercream, then carefully place it on top of the larger cake using a palette knife. Apply some buttercream to hold the cake board in place. Let set overnight.

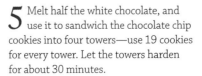

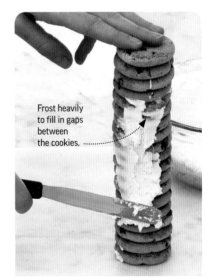

Frost heavily to fill in gaps between the cookies. ⋯⋯⋯

5 Melt half the white chocolate, and use it to sandwich the chocolate chip cookies into four towers—use 19 cookies for every tower. Let the towers harden for about 30 minutes.

6 Use the palette knife to crumb coat with a layer of ivory buttercream, filling all the gaps. Chill the towers in the fridge, and then cover with another layer of buttercream. Let set overnight.

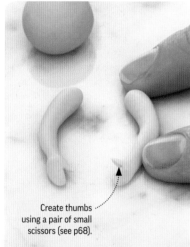

Create thumbs
using a pair of small
scissors (see p68).

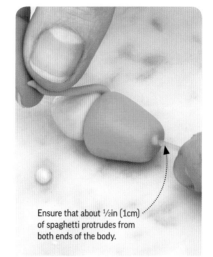

Ensure that about ½in (1cm)
of spaghetti protrudes from
both ends of the body.

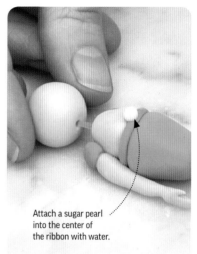

Attach a sugar pearl
into the center of
the ribbon with water.

7 To make the princess, roll the flesh fondant into a large gumball-sized ball and model into a gentle oval to form the head. Use more fondant to model a slim neck and décolletage, and two arms, gently curved at the elbow.

8 Model a tapered torso from the rose-colored fondant and attach to the décolletage using dry spaghetti. Make a thin rope of the rose fondant and wrap around the top of the torso to hide the join, affixing in place with water.

9 Create two cap sleeves from pea-sized balls of rose fondant and attach to the top of the arms with water. Affix the arms at the shoulders using a little water. Moisten the base of the head and slip onto the spaghetti.

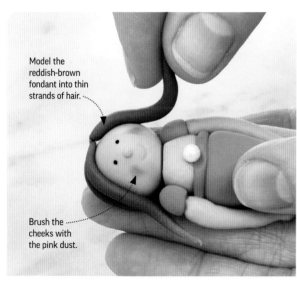

Model the
reddish-brown
fondant into thin
strands of hair.

Brush the
cheeks with
the pink dust.

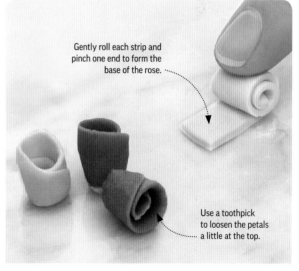

Gently roll each strip and
pinch one end to form the
base of the rose.

Use a toothpick
to loosen the petals
a little at the top.

10 Create a nose with a tiny ball of the flesh fondant, and dot two eyes with the edible black pen. Use the end of a piping nozzle to score a smile. Attach the hair with water, giving it a side part. Set three sugar pearls into the hair to create a tiara. Let set overnight.

11 Dust a surface with cornstarch and roll out some of the pale pink fondant very thinly. Carefully cut out ribbons, about ¼in (5mm) wide. Cut these to 1in (2.5cm) long pieces and roll to make about 20 small roses. Repeat with the fuchsia fondant to create 20 more roses. Set aside.

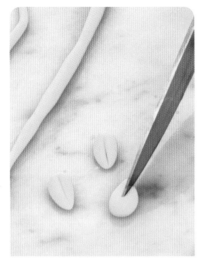

12 To make the vines, roll some of the pale-green fondant to form thin ropes. From the remaining fondant, model about 30 small teardrop-shaped leaves. Score the veins using a sharp knife. Let dry.

13 Once the cookie towers have set, place them on the cake drum around the cake tiers. Affix them using buttercream frosting, or melted white chocolate, spread on the base of each tower.

14 For the windows, dust a surface with confectioner's sugar and roll out most of the pink fondant to $^1/_{16}$–$^1/_8$in (2–3mm) thick. Use the small shield-shaped cutter to make 17 windows, and create the panes with a knife.

15 Moisten the backs of the windows with a little water, and press into place on the cakes and towers. Attach three windows on the back and front of the top tier, and attach three windows on the back of the lower tier.

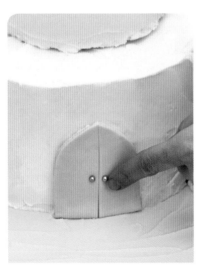

16 With the large shield-shaped cutter, create a door from the rolled-out pink fondant and score a line down the center. Affix to the cake with water and press two silver balls onto the surface with royal icing for doorknobs.

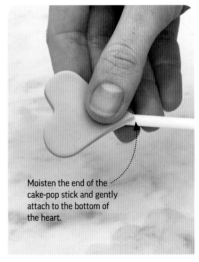

Moisten the end of the cake-pop stick and gently attach to the bottom of the heart.

17 Dust a surface with cornstarch and roll the remaining pink fondant to about $^1/_8$in (3mm) thick. Use the large heart-shaped cutter to cut out a pink heart. Attach to the cake-pop stick and let dry.

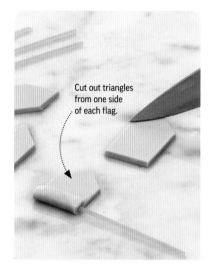

18 Cut out four flags from the rolled-out pink fondant, using a sharp knife, and attach onto four small pieces of spaghetti. Let the flags dry.

19 To make the tower tops, use the serrated knife to trim the base of the waffle cones, so that they are as even as possible. Melt the remaining white chocolate, dip the tips of the cones, one by one, into the white chocolate, and immediately roll in a small bowl of sprinkles. Let harden, and then use white chocolate to attach the cones to the tops of the towers.

20 To decorate the towers, halve the white chocolate disks covered in sprinkles and affix around the base of the cones with a little melted white chocolate. Attach another row of white chocolate buttons below the cones, using a little more melted chocolate.

21 To finish the towers, roll four small balls out of the remaining pale-green fondant and flatten at the base. Moisten the bases with a little water and press onto the tops of the cone roofs. Carefully press the flagpoles into the green tops.

Princess Castle ♡ 151

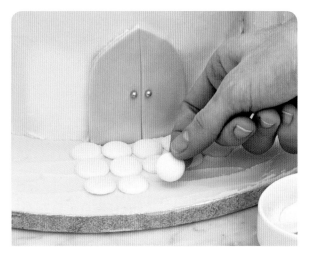

22 Soften the remaining green buttercream with a little milk, or heat in the microwave, to piping consistency. Fill a piping bag with the buttercream and dot the backs of five white chocolate buttons, one at a time. Press the buttons in front of the door to get a neat row. Repeat to get four rows.

23 Using a little royal icing, or buttercream, affix the sugar pearls around the base of both the cake tiers and the four towers to form a border around the entire castle.

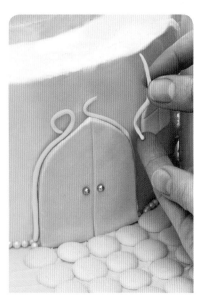

24 Brush the backs of the green vines with a little water, and press into place around the door in a decorative pattern.

25 Pipe a dot of buttercream at the base of each rose and place along the sides of the path, at the base of the front towers, on the surface of the lower tier, and around the cake drum. Affix 1–2 green leaves around some of the roses.

26 Apply buttercream onto the base of the marshmallows and stick into place around the top perimeter of each cake tier, alternating pink and white marshmallows. Attach the princess with a little water.

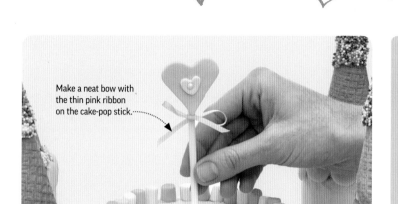

Make a neat bow with the thin pink ribbon on the cake-pop stick.

27 Dust a surface with cornstarch and roll out the white fondant very thinly. Cut out a heart, using the small heart-shaped cutter. Affix a sugar pearl into the center of the white heart using a little water. Attach the white heart to the center of the larger pink heart and press the stick into the middle of the top of the castle.

28 Let the cake set for 1 hour. Use craft glue to affix the pink satin ribbon around the base of the drum.

Hearts and Flowers Cake Pops

Create a centerpiece with these delicate, exquisite cake pops (see pp172–3) and delight your little princess. To make the heart, mold the cake pop into shape with your fingers, before dipping into pink candy melts. Roll out a little ivory fondant very thinly and use a heart-shaped cutter to cut out a small heart. Attach to the pop with a little water and decorate.

For the rose, dip the cake pop in pink candy melts and let harden. Roll pink fondant very thinly and cut out nine petal shapes, using a petal cutter. Wrap the first petal around the cake pop, so that it is almost closed at the top. Moisten the base of another petal and affix to the first one. Repeat with the other petals, moving around the cake pop, so that three petals form the inside row, and five petals are placed around that. Roll out some green fondant, cut out a calyx with a star cutter, and affix below the rose with water.

Decorate by attaching a sugar pearl in the center, or piping a dot of royal icing.

Gently separate the petals and curl the tops of the petals outward.

Flying Superhero

It's surprisingly easy to make this colorful cake, with simple buildings cut from flower paste and piped with yellow royal icing, and fondant lightning bolts, stars, and explosions attached to bright blue frosting. Decorate your superhero with colored fondant to create your child's favorite character.

PREP 1 hr 20 mins   **BAKE** 25–30 mins   **DECORATE** 4–5 hrs, plus overnight drying time   **SERVES** 20

Ingredients

- cornstarch, for dusting
- 3½oz (100g) blue-gray flower paste (see p177)
- 3½oz (100g) black flower paste
- 3½oz (100g) bright-blue flower paste
- 2 x 8in (20cm) round vanilla sponge cakes (see p164), sandwiched and crumb coated with buttercream (see p171)
- ⅔ cup (7oz/200g) buttercream frosting (see p180)
- confectioner's sugar, for dusting
- 2¼lb (1kg) bright-blue fondant (see p176)
- ¾oz (20g) flesh-colored fondant, strengthened
- dry spaghetti
- ¾oz (20g) black fondant, strengthened
- 7oz (200g) yellow fondant, strengthened
- 7oz (200g) red fondant, strengthened
- ¼ cup royal icing (see p181)
- ½ cup royal icing, tinted bright yellow

Equipment

- sharp knife
- palette knife

continued on the next page...

1 Dust a surface with cornstarch and roll out the blue-gray, black, and bright-blue flower pastes to about ¹⁄₁₆in (2mm) thick. Use a sharp knife to cut rectangles for the buildings in different sizes and shapes (2–4in/5–10cm tall), altering the angle of the tops to create an interesting skyline. Let dry on a dusted plate for 2–3 days.

2 Refrigerate the sandwiched and crumb-coated cake to set for 30 minutes, then apply a second, light coat of frosting with the palette knife (see p171). Dust a surface with confectioner's sugar and roll out the bright-blue fondant to about ¼in (5mm) thick. It should be large enough to cover the top and sides of the cake. Use the fondant smoother to achieve a neat finish (see p178). Cut off the excess at the base and let dry overnight.

- fondant roller
- fondant smoother
- modeling tool, or drinking straw
- edible black pen
- tweezers
- Dresden tool
- ball tool
- small sewing or nail scissors
- toothpick
- 10 cake-pop sticks
- 4 x 3¼in (10 x 8cm) red fabric
- needle and red thread
- 3¼ft (1m) red satin ribbon, 1¼in (3cm) wide
- craft glue
- piping bag
- small round piping tips (Wilton no. 1, 2, and 3)

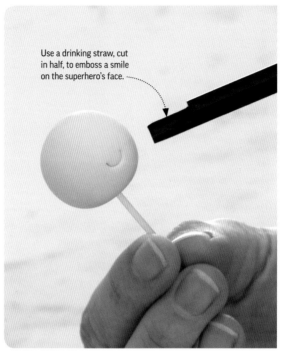

Use a drinking straw, cut in half, to emboss a smile on the superhero's face.

3 To make the superhero, roll the flesh-colored fondant into a cherry-sized ball and mold into the shape of a head. Insert a small piece of dry spaghetti into the head for support. Use a modeling tool or a drinking straw to score a smile.

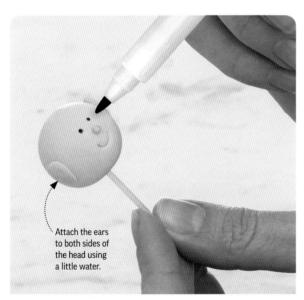

Attach the ears to both sides of the head using a little water.

Gently score the hair using a pair of tweezers.

4 Draw two eyes using the edible black pen. Roll a pin-sized ball of the flesh-colored fondant and place on the face for the nose. Roll two tiny balls of the fondant, flatten to form ears, and affix. Let dry overnight.

5 Roll a circle of fondant large enough to cover the back of the head. Shape the front to create a hairline and affix to the head using a little water. Create sideburns with extra strands. Let dry overnight.

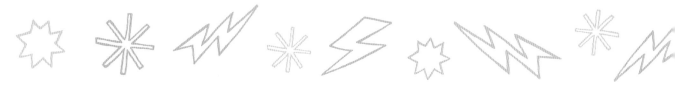

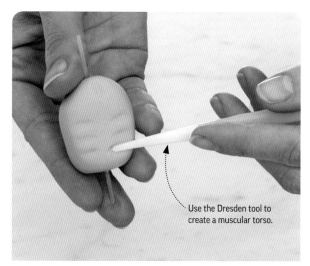

Use the Dresden tool to create a muscular torso.

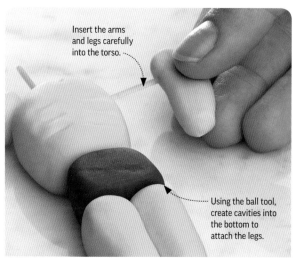

Insert the arms and legs carefully into the torso.

Using the ball tool, create cavities into the bottom to attach the legs.

6 Form the torso by modeling the yellow fondant with your fingers to create the upper body, tapering it slightly toward the waist. Cut the bottom so that it will sit flush with the hip area. Insert a small piece of dry spaghetti right through the torso for support.

7 Roll a walnut-sized ball of the red fondant and flatten from all sides to create the shorts. Attach at the base of the torso. Roll two long sausages of yellow fondant for legs and taper toward the knee, to fit into the boots later. Roll two small sausages of yellow fondant for the upper arms, tapering toward the elbow. Hold everything in place with spaghetti.

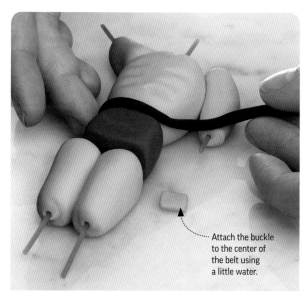

Attach the buckle to the center of the belt using a little water.

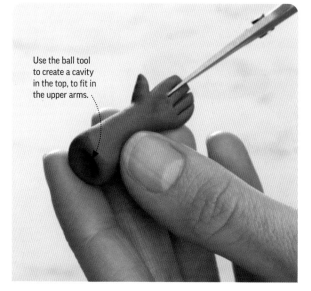

Use the ball tool to create a cavity in the top, to fit in the upper arms.

8 To make the belt, roll a thin rope of black fondant. Attach it around the superhero just above the red shorts. Make a tiny square of yellow fondant for the buckle and affix to the belt.

9 Model narrow cones of red fondant to create the gloves. Flatten one end and use small scissors to cut out the fingers. Use the toothpick as a mini rolling pin to soften the edges and define the shape. Set aside to harden slightly.

10 Model boots from two sausages of red fondant, cutting them off at the top and modeling the base to form the feet. Use the ball tool to create a cavity in the top into which the legs will fit. After a little drying time, moisten the tops of the boots with a little water and affix in place with the lengths of spaghetti. Carefully press a cake-pop stick into the top of the leg, to make a hole (see step 12 for positioning), and pull out the stick.

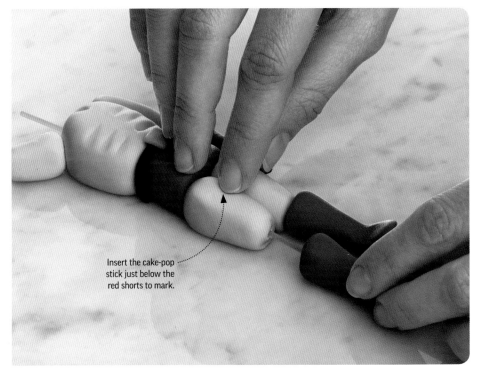

Insert the cake-pop stick just below the red shorts to mark.

11 Moisten the end of the red glove and affix to the spaghetti that is running through the arms. Once the head is dry, affix onto a pea-sized ball of strengthened yellow fondant, flattened, base moistened with water, and slipped onto the spaghetti at the top of the torso, to form a neck. Let dry overnight.

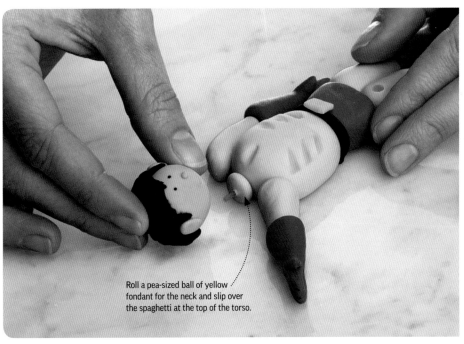

Roll a pea-sized ball of yellow fondant for the neck and slip over the spaghetti at the top of the torso.

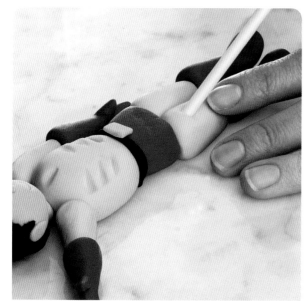

12 Apply a little royal icing to the end of a cake-pop stick and press it into the hole created in step 10.

13 Cut out a square of red fabric, and carefully gather at the top, using a needle and thread to make running stitches. Pull the thread at one end so that the fabric bunches, and tie with a knot. Cut off the excess. Affix in place with royal icing.

14 When the cake has dried fully, roll out the remaining red, orange, and yellow fondant and use a sharp knife to cut out lightning bolts and stars in different sizes. Layer different colors of stars to create an explosion effect, attaching together with water. Let dry for 1 hour.

15 Move the cake to a presentation plate, if you wish. Affix the red satin ribbon around the base of the cake using a dot of royal icing. Affix the stars and bolts onto the cake in a random pattern using a little royal icing.

16 Fill the piping bag with yellow-tinted royal icing and use a variety of tips to pipe windows on the flower-paste buildings, using dots and lines. Use a little leftover yellow fondant, rolled very thinly, to create doors, if desired.

17 Press pieces of cake-pop sticks into the cake and affix the buildings to them by piping a line of royal icing up the back of each building. Press into place on the sticks to create an interesting skyline.

Superpower Cupcakes

Create superpower treats by spreading bright-yellow buttercream over the surface of baked, cooled cupcakes (see pp174–5). While they are setting, roll out yellow, orange, and red fondant to about 1/8in (3mm) thick, on a surface dusted with confectioner's sugar. Use a sharp knife to cut starlike explosions in a variety of sizes. Let harden for 1–2 hours, and then layer the explosions, using a little water. Affix these to the surface of the cupcakes with a little buttercream.

If you have leftover fondant, you can add lightning bolts or the crest of your child's favorite superhero.

Make your flying supergirl in the same way as the superhero in different colors, with long brown hair and a fluttering cape.

18 When the superhero figure is dry, press it into the top of the cake, so that it hovers over the skyline.

Take one *cupcake...*

You can transform a basic cupcake into one of these clever creations using store-bought sweets and colored fondant. Complete a theme or tailor-make a cake for each guest.

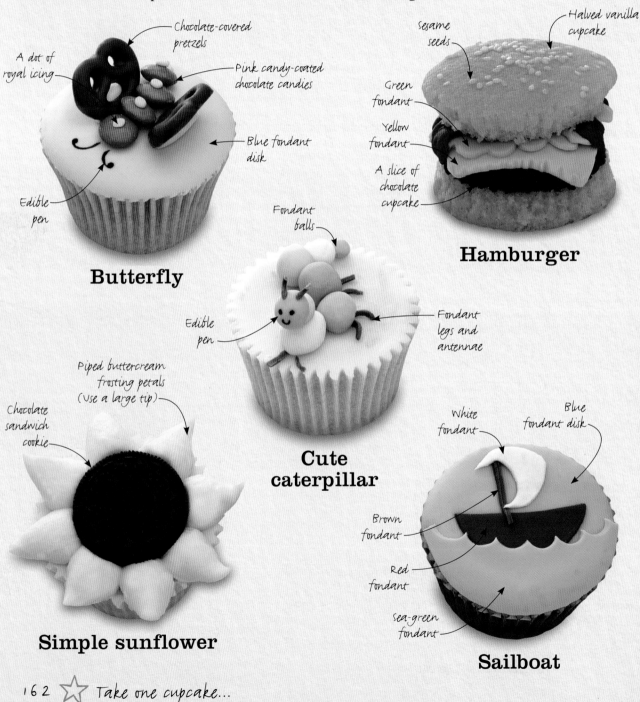

Chocolate-covered pretzels

A dot of royal icing

Pink candy-coated chocolate candies

Blue fondant disk

Edible pen

Butterfly

Fondant balls

Edible pen

Fondant legs and antennae

Cute caterpillar

sesame seeds

Halved vanilla cupcake

Green fondant

Yellow fondant

A slice of chocolate cupcake

Hamburger

Piped buttercream frosting petals (use a large tip)

Chocolate sandwich cookie

Simple sunflower

White fondant

Blue fondant disk

Brown fondant

Red fondant

sea-green fondant

Sailboat

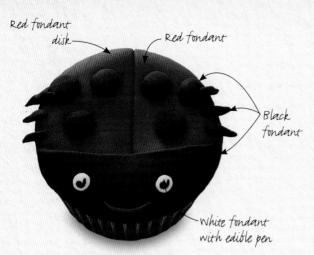

Red fondant disk

Red fondant

Black fondant

White fondant with edible pen

Ladybug

Crushed chocolate cookies

Chocolate cupcake

Gummy worms

Garden worms

Chocolate cupcake crumbs

sea-green fondant with footprint shape cut out

Prehistoric print

Yellow, black, and white fondant bee

Edible pen

Pale-brown fondant over a buttercream dome

Brown food coloring mixed with water and brushed on

Dark brown fondant

Busy bee hive

Ropes of gray fondant

Blood-red food coloring mixed with water

Gray fondant disk

Brain power

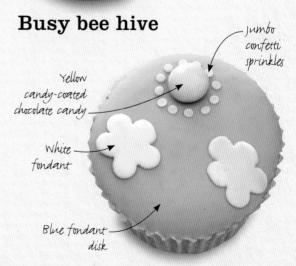

Jumbo confetti sprinkles

Yellow candy-coated chocolate candy

White fondant

Blue fondant disk

Summer sky

Sponge Cakes

A perfect cake not only looks great, but also tastes delicious. A classic sponge cake is an ideal base for most decorated cakes, and you can flavor it with a variety of natural extracts or ingredients to suit your taste. Denser cakes, like pound cake, are better for carving or heavy decorations.

Vanilla sponge cake

This sponge cake makes a good base for lots of different kinds of cakes, and can be adapted to incorporate many flavors. Use larger diameter pans for thin layers, and smaller pans for deeper ones.

 PREP 20 mins   **BAKE** 25-30 mins   **SERVES** 10/makes 12 cupcakes

Ingredients

- 1 cup unsalted butter, softened
- ½ cup granulated sugar
- 4 eggs
- 1 tsp pure vanilla extract
- 1¾ cups self-raising flour
- 1 tsp baking powder

Equipment

- electric mixer
- 2 x 8in (20cm) round cake pans, greased and lined (see p168)
- palette knife

Coloring sponge cakes

Use food coloring pastes or gels rather than liquids for vivid colors. Colors tend to deepen when baked, so add 1 teaspoon of paste or gel to the batter, blend, and check before adding more.

1 Preheat the oven to 350°F (180°C). Soften the butter and beat with the sugar in a bowl for 2 minutes, or until pale and fluffy.

3 Sift in the flour and baking powder, and gently fold in with a metal spoon, keeping the mixture light and smooth.

2 Add the eggs, one at a time, mixing well. Add the pure vanilla extract and beat for 2 minutes, until bubbles appear on the surface.

To bake

Divide the mixture evenly between the pans, smoothing the surface with a palette knife. Bake for 25–30 minutes, or until a skewer comes out clean.

To finish

Cool the cakes in the pans for 10 minutes, and then turn onto a wire rack. When completely cool, fill as desired.

Pound cake

Just a few simple ingredients are needed for this dense, buttery, lemon-flavored cake. Replace lemon zest with $1^1/_2$ teaspoon of pure vanilla extract, or any other flavor of your choice.

 PREP 20 mins   **BAKE** 50-60 mins   **SERVES** 10

Ingredients

- 1 cup unsalted butter
- 1 cup superfine sugar
- 4 eggs
- 2½ cups all-purpose flour
- grated zest of 1 lemon

Equipment

- 8in (20cm) round springform cake pan, greased and lined (see p168)

1 Preheat the oven to 350°F (180°C). Soften the butter and beat with the sugar in a bowl until fluffy. Add the eggs, one at a time, mixing well as you go.

2 Beat for 2 more minutes, until bubbles appear on the surface. Sift in the flour, add the zest, and gently fold in with a metal spoon until just smooth.

3 Spoon the batter into the pan, flatten using a palette knife, and bake for 50–60 minutes, or until a skewer comes out clean (see p169). Let cool in the pan for 10 minutes and then turn onto a wire rack to cool completely.

Chocolate cake

An all-time favorite, the yogurt in this recipe makes this cake extra moist. It is delicious when filled with chocolate or vanilla buttercream frosting.

 PREP 30 mins   **BAKE** 20-25 mins   **SERVES** 10/makes 12 cupcakes

Ingredients

- ¾ cup unsalted butter, softened
- ¾ cup packed light brown sugar
- 3 large eggs
- ¾ cup all-purpose flour
- ½ cup cocoa powder
- 1 tsp baking powder
- 2 tbsp Greek yogurt

Equipment

- 2 x 8in (20cm) round cake pans, greased and lined (see p168)

1 Preheat the oven to 350°F (180°C). Soften the butter and beat with the sugar in a bowl until light and fluffy. Add the eggs, one at a time, mixing well.

2 In a separate bowl, sift together all the dry ingredients. Fold the flour mixture into the batter with a metal spoon until well blended. When the batter is light and fluffy, gently fold in the yogurt.

3 Divide the mixture evenly between the pans and bake for 20–25 minutes. Cool the cakes in the pans for 10 minutes, and then turn onto a wire rack. When completely cool, fill as desired.

Red velvet cake

This vivid red cake is traditionally topped with cream-cheese buttercream frosting. Boiled beets give this cake its color, but you can also use red food coloring paste alongside the beets, if desired.

 PREP 50 mins   **BAKE** 35 mins   **SERVES** 10

Ingredients

- 3–4 medium beets, 1lb 2oz (500g) in total
- 2¼ cups all-purpose flour
- ½ cup cocoa powder
- 2 tsp baking soda
- ½ tsp salt
- ¾ cup unsalted butter, softened
- 1¼ cups brown sugar
- ¾ cup granulated sugar
- 3 large eggs, at room temperature
- 2 tsp pure vanilla extract
- 3½oz (100g) dark chocolate, broken into pieces and melted
- ⅔ cup buttermilk mixed with 2 tsp cider vinegar
- cream-cheese buttercream frosting (optional)

Equipment

- 2 x 8in (20cm) round cake pans, greased and lined (see p168)

1 Cook the beets in a pan half-filled with water for 30–40 minutes. Cool, then peel. Preheat the oven to 350°F (180°C).

2 Purée the beets in a food processor, adding a little water if needed. Sift together the flour, cocoa, baking soda, and salt.

To bake

Slowly add the flour mixture and buttermilk-vinegar mix to the batter. Beat well. Stir in 1 cup of the beet purée, and mix well together. Divide the batter between the pans and bake for 35 minutes.

To finish

Cool and slice each cake in half horizontally. Layer the cake with cream cheese buttercream frosting, if desired.

3 In a separate bowl, beat the butter, sugars, eggs, and pure vanilla extract, then add the cooled, melted chocolate. Stir to form a uniform mixture.

Carrot cake

This rich, moist cake is easy to make and works well in stacked and layered projects because its density helps support weight. Cream-cheese buttercream frosting makes for a perfect topping.

 PREP 20 mins   **BAKE** 45 mins   **SERVES** 10

Ingredients

- 1 cup walnuts
- 1 cup sunflower oil
- 3 large eggs
- 1 cup packed light brown sugar
- 1 tsp pure vanilla extract
- 1¼ cups carrots, about 7oz (200g)
- ¾ cup golden raisins
- 1⅓ cups self-rising flour, sifted
- ⅓ cup whole wheat flour, sifted
- pinch of salt
- 1 tsp ground cinnamon
- 1 tsp ground ginger
- ¼ tsp grated nutmeg
- grated zest of 1 orange

Equipment

- 9in (23cm) round springform cake pan, greased and lined (see p168)

Walnuts add great flavor and texture to cakes.

1 Preheat the oven to 350°F (180°C). Roast the walnuts for 5 minutes, rub with a dish towel, and roughly chop.

3 Squeeze the carrots dry and fold into the batter. Add the walnuts and golden raisins, stir in the remaining ingredients, and mix.

2 Pour the oil and crack the eggs into a bowl. Add the sugar and pure vanilla extract, and beat until smooth and thick in consistency.

To bake

Spread the batter into the pan, using a palette knife to smooth. Bake for 45 minutes, or until a skewer comes out clean (see p169).

To finish

Cool for 10 minutes in the pan, and then transfer to a wire rack to cool completely. If desired, slice horizontally and fill, or frost the top, with cream-cheese buttercream frosting.

Preparing a Cake

It is always worth taking your time to prepare your pans carefully to ensure even cooking of the cake and prevent it from sticking. Test with a skewer before removing from the oven, and always cool cakes on a rack before frosting, filling, or decorating.

Preparing pans

Greasing Almost all cake pans, including nonstick pans, should be greased with butter, margarine, or oil. Use a pastry brush to ensure even coverage. Molded pans, especially novelty pans, need to be greased particularly well in the corners and crevices.

Dusting Sprinkle 1 tablespoon of all-purpose flour into the bottom of the pan. Hold the pan over the sink, tilt it to move the flour from side to side, and tap the bottom to ensure even coverage. Discard unused flour.

Lining Using parchment paper helps to prevent burning, particularly for cakes with longer cooking times. Make sure the parchment paper is smooth to avoid creating ridges in the cake.

1 Grease the pans well to ensure that the parchment paper sticks to the pan and does not move when the batter is poured.

2 Cut a strip of the parchment paper slightly longer than the circumference and slightly wider than the height of the pan. This ensures none of the batter goes through the parchment paper strips.

3 Fold the strip about 1in (2.5cm) from the long edge and make some evenly spaced cuts to the fold line using kitchen scissors.

4 Press the strip into the inside edge of the pan. Cut a circle from the parchment paper, using the bottom of the pan as a template, and fit in the base of the pan.

Baking and cooling

Make sure that cakes are cooked at the right temperature and for the correct length of time before you remove them from the oven. This ensures good consistency and optimum rising.

Baking Preheat the oven for 20 minutes before baking. Fan or convection ovens require a lower temperature than conventional ovens. If the recipe does not specify this, reduce the temperature by about 25°F (20°C). Pour the batter into the greased and lined pans and smooth the surface using a palette knife. Knock the pan gently against a hard surface before it goes into the oven, to release air bubbles. Don't open the oven—changes in temperature sometimes cause cakes to sink or to rise unevenly. If your oven heats unevenly, turn the cake after three-quarters of the cooking time. Cook for the entire time suggested by the recipe.

Testing There are two main ways to test a cake. The first is to press gently down in the center of the cake with your finger. If it springs back, chances are it is ready. To be certain, insert a metal or wooden skewer into the center of the cake. If it comes out clean, the cake is ready. Cakes in novelty pans can take longer to bake, so be sure to check the recommended time on the recipe provided on the pan packaging.

Cooling Cool a cake in its pan for about 10 minutes (a little longer if it is a deep, large cake), to help the cake keep its shape and "set." Then turn it onto one wire rack and invert it onto another rack to cool completely. The base of your cake should be on the rack, not the top, to prevent it from losing its height and texture. Always make sure the cake is completely cool before frosting and plating it, as this will prevent crumbling, breakage, and movement. If you are in a hurry, you can chill your cake after it has been cooled in the pan.

Leveling

For a perfect finish, it is important to level your cake. Cool the cakes in the pan for 10 minutes before trimming the uneven parts. If your cake is lopsided or lumpy, cool completely before leveling.

Turntable method

Place the cake on a cake drum, and then on top of a turntable or lazy Susan. If it is not the drum you will be using for the finished cake, dust it first with confectioner's sugar to ensure that the cake will not stick. Use a ruler and toothpicks pressed into the cake to mark your cutting line, to be sure it is even all the way around. Carefully turn the stand and gently move a serrated knife back and forth in a sawing motion to remove the dome, or any lumps, until you have a completely flat surface. Some people find it easier to freeze the cakes partially before leveling, which prevents chunks of cake from being drawn up when you "saw" through it.

Cake leveler method

If you have a cake leveler, place the cake on a cake drum, over a firm surface, and carefully position the blade at the appropriate height. Gently saw into the side using a back and forth motion. Once you have gotten past the crust, simply glide the blade through the cake to the other side. If you are finding it tricky to keep the cake still while you cut, you can place it on a drum exactly the same size as the cake and put the cake, on the drum, back into the cake pan. Level across the cake using the top edge of the pan.

Sandwiching

Sandwich thin layers of sponge cake to make it easier to carve. Ganache, whipped cream, and jam can also be used as fillings. For best results, let the filling set before frosting the cake.

Ingredients

- cooled cake layers, leveled
- buttercream frosting (see p180)

Equipment

- cake drum
- turntable or lazy Susan
- piping bag with large, round tip
- palette knife

1 Move the base layer of the cake onto a drum and then onto a turntable. Fill the piping bag with frosting and pipe around the inside edge. Place a spoonful of frosting in the center and spread with a palette knife.

2 Place the next layer on top, leveled side down. For two-layered cakes, you are now ready to crumb coat and frost. To build the cake higher, repeat, and finish with a leveled-side down layer, for a level surface.

Crumb coating

Crumb coating is like adding a base coat to a wall before painting. It smoothes over any cracks or holes in the surface and helps the cake stay sealed and moist.

Ingredients

- 4 cakes, leveled, and layers filled with buttercream frosting
- buttercream frosting (see p180), thinned with a little milk

Equipment

- cake drum
- turntable or lazy Susan
- palette knife

1 Place the cake on a drum on a turntable. Use a palette knife to apply a thin layer of buttercream onto the cake. Start at the top of the cake and swirl the buttercream over the surface as you turn it around on the turntable.

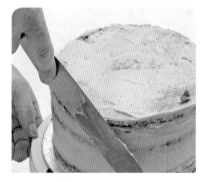

2 Spread the frosting around the sides until evenly covered. A few crumbs may be embedded in the frosting, which is normal. Refrigerate, or let set for up to 2 hours. Apply the final layer of frosting or fondant (see p178 and p182).

Cake Pops

Cake pops are not only easy to make, but delicious too. Use them to accessorize cakes or to create treats for party bags. There are two main ways to make cake pops: the method below uses up leftover cake or you can also use a pan to make your cake pops.

Using baked cake

Use whole cakes or leftover sponge cake to make perfect cake pops. This method works best for cake pops that are molded into novelty shapes or simple balls. Make sure they are firm before dipping.

PREP 10 mins, plus cooling

MAKES 20-25

Ingredients
- 4 cups chocolate cake (see p164)
- ½ cup buttercream frosting (see p180)

Insert cake-pop sticks into the balls and let set before dipping.

1 Purée the whole cake, or leftover cake, in a food processor to create crumbs.

2 Place the cake crumbs in a bowl. Stir in the buttercream and mix until you get a smooth dough.

3 Using your hands, gently mold the cake mixture into uniform walnut-sized balls.

4 Place on a plate, with space between each, and refrigerate for 3 hours; or freeze them for 30 minutes.

Cake-pop pans

Use cake-pop pans to make uniform balls that are ready to dip and decorate. Dense pound cakes work better for making cake pops.

 PREP
20 mins

 BAKE
15–18 mins

 MAKES
12

Ingredients
- butter or oil, for greasing
- all-purpose flour, for dusting
- ½ quantity pound cake batter (see p165)

Equipment
- 12-hole cake-pop pan
- skewer

1 Preheat the oven to 350°F (180°C). Grease and dust the pans. Spoon the batter into the bottom half of the pan (without holes) so that it mounds over the top of the pan. Cake-pop pans differ, so follow the instructions to ensure you use the correct amount of batter.

2 Place the top half of the pan on top and secure. Bake for 15–18 minutes. After baking time, test every 2 minutes with a skewer. Let the cakes cool in the pan for 10 minutes, and then turn onto a wire rack to cool completely.

3 Chill the cake pops before decorating so that they keep their shape.

Coating cake pops

Dip cake pops in candy melts or melted chocolate to provide a firm coating and the perfect canvas for decorating.

Ingredients
- melted chocolate
- 12 cake pops
- 7oz (200g) candy melts

Equipment
- 12 cake-pop sticks
- styrofoam

1 Dip one end of a cake-pop stick into a little melted chocolate and insert into the center of a cake pop. Repeat with the remaining cake pops. Stand the cake pops upright in a piece of styrofoam, or an overturned colander, and chill for 20–30 minutes.

2 Melt the white candy melts. Dip cake pops into the melted candy, coating evenly. Allow excess to drip off.

3 Stand the cake pops upright in a piece of styrofoam, or an overturned colander, for 30 minutes, or until they harden.

Cupcakes

Cupcakes are ideal for parties, creating very little mess and requiring no plates. They can be frosted with buttercream, topped with fondant, or simply filled and dusted with confectioner's sugar. Make sure they are completely cool before decorating.

Preparing

Be sure not to overfill the liners, and cook for the correct length of time. Always preheat the oven for at least 20 minutes and prepare the pans before you begin to make the batter (see p164).

Using liners

Cupcake liners add a decorative element, make the cupcakes look neater, and help them remain fresh and moist for longer. If you choose to use a cupcake pan on its own, grease and dust it, brush with cake release products, or spray with a nonstick baking spray. Silicone cases do not require a cupcake pan. Fill and set them upright on a baking sheet. Grease and dust them with all-purpose flour to ensure that the cupcakes do not stick.

Filling

Fill the cupcake liners or pans about two-thirds full. Do not overfill or they will spill over the sides or develop a "nose." Standard-sized cupcakes require about $^1/_3$ cup of batter. For mini cupcakes, a heaping tablespoon of batter is enough. For special effects, layer different colors of batter into the liners with a piping bag. Create a surprise center by putting candies, or even a cookie or a miniature brownie, into the center before baking.

Baking

A standard-sized cupcake will take 18–20 minutes to bake, while mini cupcakes will take 8–10 minutes. They are ready if a skewer inserted in the middle of the cake comes out clean. When baking several pans at the same time, increase the baking time by a few minutes, and rotate the sheets halfway through. Allow to cool in the pan for at least 10 minutes, and then cool on a wire rack. If you did not use liners, turn the cupcakes onto your hand before placing them on the rack.

Piping

Cupcakes can be frosted with a palette knife or, for a more professional finish, piped using one of a variety of tips fitted onto a pastry or piping bag.

Ingredients
- medium-consistency buttercream frosting (see p180)
- cooled cupcakes

Equipment
- piping bag with large open-star tip

1 Attach the tip to the piping bag and half-fill with the frosting, so that the bag is easy to handle. Hold the tip ½in (1cm) above the cupcake at a 90° angle and pipe from the outside edge inward, in a spiral.

2 Apply pressure evenly. Slowly increase the pressure at the center, so that the frosting forms a peak. Release the pressure to end the spiral at the center of the cupcake.

Filling

Cupcakes can be filled with jam, buttercream frosting, whipped cream, or even peanut butter, fruit mousses, and curds. Add a marshmallow or another treat before baking for an extra surprise.

Cone method

With a sharp paring knife, cut out a cone shape from the center of each cupcake. Slice off the tip of the cone and set aside. Spoon the filling of your choice into the cavity, stopping just before the top. Replace the lid and frost, as shown above.

Piping method

If you have thin, smooth frosting or jam, you can use a plain round tip or a specialized injector tip on a piping bag. Attach the tip, load the piping bag with filling, and then insert it into the center of the cupcake from the top. Gently press on the bag while piping, until the filling begins to expand out of the insertion hole. Frost and decorate as usual.

Fondant

This classic recipe works well both to cover cakes and to create decorations. Use food coloring paste to tint the fondant, bearing in mind that the color deepens over time.

 PREP 20 mins   **MAKES** 2lbs 3oz (1kg)

Ingredients

- 2 sheets gelatin
- ½ cup liquid glucose
- 1 tbsp glycerine
- 9 cups confectioner's sugar, plus extra for dusting
- food coloring paste (optional)

Equipment

- toothpick

1 Soak the gelatin sheets in cold water for 10 minutes. Wring dry and slowly dissolve in ½ cup warm water. Mix in the glucose and glycerine until well blended. Set aside.

2 Sift the sugar into a separate bowl. Create a well in the center and pour in the liquid gelatin mix a little at a time. Stir to form a soft ball.

strengthening fondant

For pliable fondant that hardens quickly without cracking, add 1 teaspoon tylose powder to every 7oz (200g) fondant.

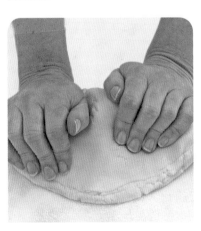

3 Dust a surface with confectioner's sugar and place the fondant onto it. Knead the fondant until it is smooth and pliable, adding water if it is too dry or confectioner's sugar if it is too tacky.

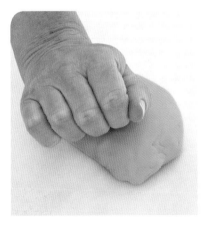

4 To color the fondant, use a toothpick to apply a little food coloring paste to the surface. Fold the fondant over the paste and then knead until it has a uniform color throughout.

Flower paste

Flower paste dries harder than fondant and can be rolled very thin for decorations, such as flowers. Although it is edible, it is not normally eaten. Color it in the same way as the fondant.

PREP 30 mins, plus thickening and chilling

MAKES 1lb 2oz (500g)

Ingredients

- 2 tsp gelatin powder, dissolved in 5 tsp warm water and allowed to thicken for 30 minutes
- 2 tsp vegetable shortening
- 2 tsp liquid glucose
- 4 cups confectioner's sugar, sifted, plus extra for dusting
- 4 tsp tylose powder
- 1 egg white
- food coloring paste (optional)

Equipment

- electric mixer

1 Place the thickened gelatin in a pan with the vegetable shortening and glucose. Stir over low heat until the liquid is clear.

2 Transfer to the bowl and beat in the confectioner's sugar, tylose, and egg white. Turn the mixer up to the highest setting.

Softening

Store flower paste in an airtight container. If the paste is sticky, add more vegetable shortening until smooth and pliable. If it is too hard and crumbly, add more beaten egg white.

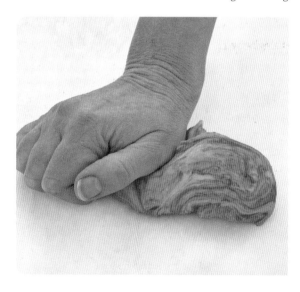

3 Continue to mix until stringy and white. Refrigerate the mixture for 1–2 days. Dust a surface with confectioner's sugar and knead the mixture until it is smooth and pliable. Color the paste in the same way as fondant (see opposite).

Covering a cake

A fondant covering provides a lovely canvas for decorations. Fondant can be applied over ganache, buttercream, or marzipan. The rolled fondant should be thick enough that it does not tear.

Ingredients

- confectioner's sugar, for dusting
- 2lb 3oz (1kg) fondant (see p176)
- 9in (23cm) 2-layer cake, crumb coated with buttercream (see p171)

Equipment

- fondant roller
- cake drum
- fondant smoother, plus one extra (optional)
- sharp knife

1 Dust a surface with confectioner's sugar. Knead and roll the fondant into a circle that can cover the top and sides of the cake with 2in (5cm) extra around the edges.

2 Cover the cake with the fondant sheet and smooth it across the top with a smoother, easing it down with your hands.

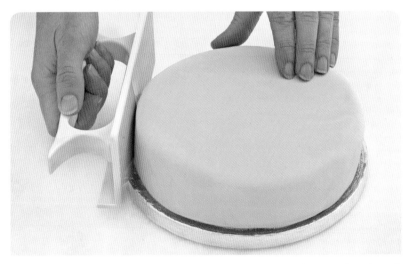

3 Trim off the excess fondant. Press the smoother evenly over the top of the cake and then run it down and around the sides of the cake until perfectly smooth. To get a sharp edge at the top of the cake, you can use two smoothers at the same time, one on the top and the other on the sides, pressing them together at the edge.

Covering a cake drum

Cover cake drums in fondant, using various colors. You can emboss the fondant, add stripes or other detail, and even paint or dust it—set overnight before placing the cake on top.

Ingredients
- cornstarch, for dusting
- 2lb 2oz (1kg) fondant, strengthened (see p176)
- tylose powder

Equipment
- fondant roller
- pastry brush
- cake drum
- fondant smoother
- sharp knife
- edible glue
- edible or fabric ribbon

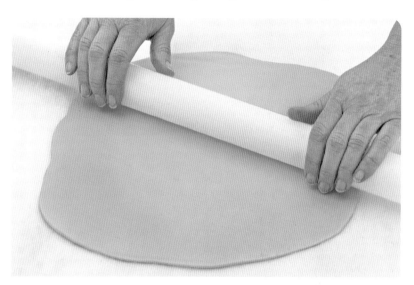

1 Dust a surface with cornstarch and roll out the fondant into a circle ¹/₁₆in (2mm) thick and 12in (30cm) in diameter.

2 Use a pastry brush to apply a little water to the top and sides of the cake drum.

3 Lift the fondant onto the drum. Use a smoother to smooth from the center outward and around the sides. Trim off any excess fondant around the base. Let set overnight before placing your cake on top.

Frosting

Vanilla buttercream frosting

This traditional buttercream frosting is softer and easier to spread than most frostings. Its rich vanilla flavor and versatile consistency make it ideal for crumb coating, frosting, and piping.

 PREP 15-20 mins   **MAKES** 1lb 10oz (750g)

Ingredients
- 1 cup unsalted butter, softened
- 2 tsp pure vanilla extract
- 5 cups confectioner's sugar
- 2 tbsp half and half or milk, plus extra for thinning if needed
- food coloring paste (optional)

Equipment
- electric mixer
- toothpick
- palette knife, for testing

1 Cream the butter and pure vanilla extract with an electric mixer. Add the confectioner's sugar. Finally, add in the half and half or milk and keep mixing until the frosting is light and fluffy.

2 Transfer the mix to a bowl. Dip a toothpick into the food coloring paste, if using. Add just a dot of the food coloring paste, a little at a time, until you achieve a uniform color.

Coloring buttercream

Use food coloring paste or gel rather than liquid colors to achieve a good consistency. The colors deepen over time, so use a tiny dab and blend before adding more.

3 The frosting should be firm enough to hold a knife upright, but soft enough to be piped.

Chocolate buttercream

This frosting works well with dark chocolate cakes. Follow step 1 of the vanilla buttercream recipe, using milk, not half and half. Add $3/4$ cup of cocoa powder with the confectioner's sugar and beat until fluffy. If you prefer a lighter flavor, halve the amount of cocoa powder and add a little more confectioner's sugar.

Royal icing

This is the perfect recipe for royal icing that can be thinned slightly for detailed piping work, or used as glue for fondant decorations.

 PREP 20 mins   **MAKES** 1lb 9oz (700g)

Ingredients
- 3 large free-range pasteurized egg whites
- 1 tsp lemon juice, plus extra if needed
- 6 cups confectioner's sugar, sifted
- food coloring paste (optional)

Equipment
- electric mixer
- toothpick

1 Beat the egg whites in a bowl and stir in the lemon juice. Gradually add the confectioner's sugar and beat well.

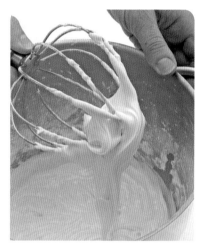

2 Beat until the icing has a smooth, toothpastelike texture. Add more lemon juice if it is too thick.

Piping
Fill your piping bag with royal icing and keep the rest covered with a damp towel to prevent it from hardening. You may need to beat it again if it separates or a crust forms.

3 Dip a toothpick into the food coloring paste, if using. Add a dot of coloring paste at a time, since a little goes a long way. Mix into the royal icing and stir until you achieve a uniform color. The icing will last for 2 weeks if it is kept covered and refrigerated.

Frosting a cake

This method of frosting can be used for buttercream, whipped cream, or ganache. Use side scrapers to achieve a smooth or textured surface, or spread in swirls with a palette knife.

Ingredients
- cake, leveled, layered, and crumb coated (see pp170–171)
- buttercream frosting (see p180)

Equipment
- cake board
- turntable or lazy Susan
- palette knife
- side scraper, flat-edged (optional)
- untextured paper towels

1 Carefully center the crumb-coated cake on top of the cake board. Place it on a turntable and spoon a large amount of buttercream frosting onto the center of the cake.

2 With a palette knife, swirl and smooth the frosting, spreading it outward and over the sides as you go.

3 Turn the cake as you spread the frosting down and around the sides of the cake to cover it as evenly as possible. When it is smooth, let cake set for about 10 minutes, and then repeat.

4 Fill a pitcher with boiling water and insert the palette knife into it. When the knife is hot, dry it and run it around the sides, turning the cake around, with the flat surface of the knife against the frosting. Repeat until smooth.

5 Fill in any gaps with extra frosting. Work on smoothing the top, turning the cake with the flat surface of the knife against the frosting. Move from one side of the cake to the other, until it is smooth.

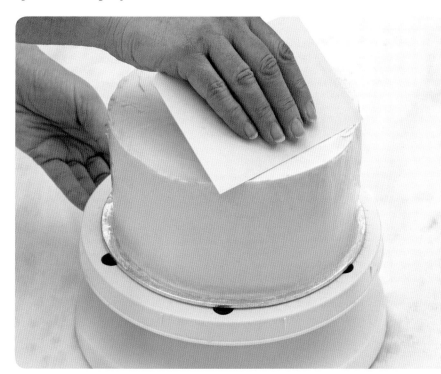

6 Alternatively, use the side scraper to smooth the frosting first on the top, then dragging any excess frosting down the sides. Smooth the sides in a single motion all the way around the cake.

Setting

Always allow buttercream frosting to set for at least 30 minutes before decorating, and even overnight, to create a really firm surface for your cake creations.

Tools and Equipment

You can use these widely available specialized tools and equipment to achieve different effects, textures, decorative touches, and perfect finishes for your birthday cakes. Start with the essentials and build your toolkit from there.

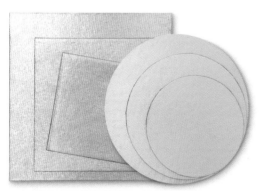

Cake boards and drums are available in different shapes and sizes. Thin cake boards support individual cakes for multiple tiers, and thicker drums provide a sturdy base.

Piping bags come in a variety of sizes. Choose larger ones to pipe buttercream frosting on cakes or cupcakes, and smaller ones for more detailed work with royal icing.

Stitching (quilting) tools are used to emboss decorations and cakes with stitching effects.

Fondant rollers are essential for ensuring that fondant, flower paste, and other modeling clays are smooth and evenly rolled.

Metal cutters help cut accurate shapes that can be layered or used as the basis for decorations. Many come in sets of multiple sizes.

Plunger cutters create crisp shapes that are released with the touch of a button. Some also emboss the surface.

Round piping tips are versatile and widely used. They come in many sizes, from tiny tips for piping dots to wider tips for prominent effects.

Petal piping tips are available in many sizes, and help to create flower petals, as well as ruffles, drapes, swags, and bows with royal or buttercream frosting.

Open star piping tips are perfect for piped borders, single drops of stars and flowers, and swirled cupcakes.

Frosting scrapers, with different edges, help to achieve a smooth or textured finish with buttercream or royal icing.

Paintbrushes come in many shapes and sizes. Use small brushes for fine details and larger ones for painting expanses of color and dusting. Choose synthetic paintbrushes that will not lose their bristles.

Dowels are cut to size and used to support heavy decorations or multiple cake tiers.

Cake-pop sticks come in different lengths and are used to support decorations.

Multi-ribbon cutters make cutting accurate lengths and strips of fondant or other pastes easy. Choose the width and affix the frame with interchangeable cutters that can emboss and/or cut decorative edges.

Flower picks are hygienic tools to help you insert fresh or wired floral decorations into the surface of a cake.

Fondant smoothers smooth decorations, boards, or cake toppings. Use two to achieve crisp corners and edges.

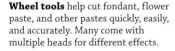

Ball tools can thin and soften edges to create natural petal shapes and contours.

Veining tools, also known as Dresden tools, add detail to fondant or paste decorations.

Wheel tools help cut fondant, flower paste, and other pastes quickly, easily, and accurately. Many come with multiple heads for different effects.

Edible felt-tip pens come in numerous colors and with different-sized tips for fine or bold painting or lettering.

Shell and blade tools help create shell patterns and textures for decorations.

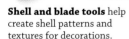

Florist's wire comes in a variety of different "gauges." Use it to produce sprays of decorations, such as hearts or stars, and to wire flowers and foliage.

Adapting Quantities

To adapt recipes for cakes of any size and shape, multiply the batches of batter you make. Check the packaging that came with novelty pans to ensure that you make the correct amount of batter and bake for the appropriate period of time.

	Cake pan	Multiple of vanilla sponge cake recipe	Fondant to cover	Bake time for sponge cake recipe at 350°F (180°C)
Round pans	5½ x 2½in (13 x 6cm)	1	14oz (400g)	15–20 mins
	6 x 2½in (15 x 6cm)	1	1lb 2oz (500g)	20–35 mins
	7 x 2¾in (18 x 7cm)	1½	1lb 8oz (700g)	30–35 mins
	8 x 3in (20 x 7.5cm)	2	1lb 12oz (800g)	35–40 mins
	9 x 3¼in (23 x 8cm)	2½	2lb (900g)	40–45 mins
	10 x 3½in (26 x 9cm)	3½	2lb 8oz (1.1kg)	50–55 mins
Square pans	6 x 2½in (15 x 6cm)	1½	1lb 8oz (700g)	30–35 mins
	7 x 2¾in (18 x 7cm)	2	1lb 12oz (800g)	35–40 mins
	8 x 3in (20 x 7.5cm)	2½	2lb (900g)	40–45 mins
	9 x 3¼in (23 x 8cm)	3½	2lb 8oz (1.1kg)	50–55 mins
	10 x 3½in (25.5 x 9cm)	5	2lb 12oz (1.25kg)	1 hr–1 hr 5 mins
	11 x 3¾in (28 x 9.5cm)	5	3lb 8oz (1.5kg)	1 hr 5 mins–1 hr 10 mins
	12 x 4in (30 x 10cm)	6	4lb 8oz (2kg)	1 hr 10 mins
Bowl (hemisphere) pans	4in (10cm)	1	14oz (400g)	40–50 mins
	6in (15cm)	2	1lb 2oz (500g)	45–60 mins
	8in (20cm)	3½	1lb 10oz (750g)	1–1¼ hrs

Templates

Use these simple templates to achieve accurate patterns for your birthday cakes and decorations. Enlarge the templates according to the percentage given here, using a photocopier or scanner, then print and cut them out, or trace and enlarge the templates by hand.

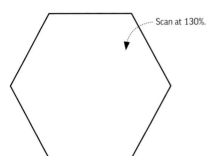

Scan at 130%.

Hexagon shape Scan, cut out, and use to cover the soccer ball in the Soccer Mania cake (p96).

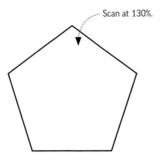

Scan at 130%.

Pentagon shape Scan, cut out, and use to cover the soccer ball in the Soccer Mania cake (p96).

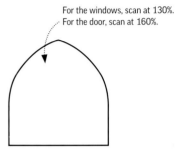

For the windows, scan at 130%. For the door, scan at 160%.

Window shape Scan, cut out, and use to create windows and doors for the Princess Castle cake (p146).

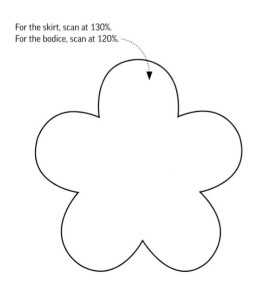

For the skirt, scan at 130%. For the bodice, scan at 120%.

Flower shape Scan, cut out, and create floral skirts for the fairies in the Pretty Fairies cake (p20).

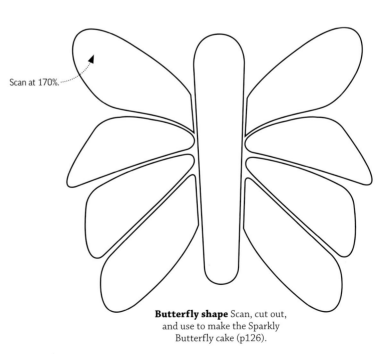

Scan at 170%.

Butterfly shape Scan, cut out, and use to make the Sparkly Butterfly cake (p126).

Index

Acknowledgments

Author's acknowledgments

It has been a great pleasure to work with such a talented and inspiring group of people on this book. In particular, I'd like to thank our brilliant team of cakemakers: Sandra Monger, Kasey Clark, Hannah Wiltshire, Felicity Dodsworth and Krystle Drewry. Their gorgeous cakes, cupcakes, and cake pops speak for themselves. Sandra was responsible for supervising most of the step-by-step photography and was completely invaluable. Huge thanks also go to inspired editor Kathy Woolley and endlessly creative designer Harriet Yeomans. Thanks also to Peggy Vance, Dawn Henderson, Christine Keilty, and the DK team for faith and brilliance.

DK would like to thank Karen Sullivan, Sandra Monger, Hannah Wiltshire, Kasey Clarke, Felicity Dodsworth and Krystle Drewry for their cake contributions.
They would also like to thank:

Photography Ian O'Leary
Art Direction Susan Downing
Prop styling Isabel de Cordova
Hand model Jenny Volich
Proofreading Claire Cross
Indexing Vanessa Bird

About the contributors

Karen Sullivan is a custom cake-maker with a successful celebration cake business. She learned to bake as a toddler, in her grandmother's kitchen in Canada, and has honed her decorating skills over the years. She creates unique and highly sought-after cakes for a range of customers and occasions.

Sandra Monger is an award-winning cake designer who specializes in custom celebration cakes. Professionally trained in advanced pâtisserie and sugar craft, she also teaches cake-decorating courses.
www.sandramongercakes.co.uk

Hannah Wiltshire is a writer and cake expert with a particular interest in beautiful baking. She runs her cake business, Baby Cakes, from her home in Bath, England. She was a judge at the Cake and Bake Show in Earls Court, London.
www.bathbabycakes.com

Kasey Clarke created Kupkase in her family kitchen, and it has since grown into a nationwide business. She's been a finalist at the National Cupcake Awards and has designed unique celebration cakes for a mix of high-profile clients and celebrities.
www.kupkase.com

Juniper Cakery is owned by Felicity Dodsworth and Krystle Drewry in Kingston upon Hull, England. Along with their head baker, Carol, they create custom celebration cakes and party confections, specializing in delicious cupcakes. They've designed and baked creations for Tala and The Happy Egg Co.
www.junipercakery.co.uk